A GIFT FOR:

....

FROM:

....

DATE:

....

GREAT
IS THY
FAITHFULNESS

52 Reasons to Trust God When Hope Feels Lost

Robert J. Morgan

Thomas Nelson
Since 1798

To Apurva and Sara

CONTENTS

INTRODUCTION

Lines of Faithfulness

O nce, when I was younger, I backed off of a perfectly good cliff, gripping a rope that was tied to a tree and hoping it wouldn't break. The forty or so yards down seemed like the Grand Canyon to me. Inching my way down the side of the cliff, I fought a sense of panic about the rope's integrity. I knew it had been tested, inspected, and adequately secured—and I was well harnessed. But my mind kept imagining the rope snapping like a string, plunging me backward to the ground. I was never really in danger, but it didn't *feel* that way.

Later I recalled several biblical characters who had similar experiences, and I wondered if they had felt as I had. The two spies in Jericho escaped when Rahab lowered them down the city walls from a high window, using a scarlet rope (Joshua 2:18). Perhaps they rappelled down like today's special forces. When David was trapped by a hostile army, his wife lowered him through a window to the ground, enabling him to escape (1 Samuel 19:12). And when Paul's life was threatened in Damascus, his friends found a large basket, tied a rope to it, and hid him inside it. As they lowered it to the ground in the dark of night, it probably bounced against every stone (Acts 9:25; 2 Corinthians 11:32–33).

None of those incidents came to mind as I scaled down the cliff. But one thing *did* enter my mind in the moment—that *faith* is trusting in the *facts* I know, not in the *feelings* I have.

That was when the experience became exhilarating.

Whenever you're dangling over difficulties or suspended on the bluffs of life, you simply must trust God's facts more than your own feelings.

And the fact is—God is faithful.

We all have ups and downs, punctuated by moments of panic. But our heavenly Father lowers us into our daily tasks and lifts us from our anxious cares by a durable cable woven from thousands of lines of biblical promises. There is a promise in the Bible for every concern you'll ever have, every need you'll ever face, every burden you'll ever bear, and every challenge you'll ever confront. You can hang on to every word.

Every scripture is precise and precious. Each word is trustworthy and true. Not the smallest strand of God's rope can fray, nor can a promise be broken. It's secured to the unshakable nature of God Almighty and guaranteed by the resurrection of Jesus Christ.

When we speak of God's faithfulness, we're talking about His integrity, dependability, and utter infallibility. He longs to give us His promises because of His unassailable love, and He intends to keep them through His infallible strength. His ropes will never break.

So, "let us hold unswervingly to the hope we profess, for he who promised is faithful" (Hebrews 10:23).

According to my count, there are nearly one hundred times in the Bible when the words *faithful* or *faithfulness* describe our Lord. I've chosen fifty-two of those passages to show you that when it feels you're at the end of your *rope*, you're not at the end of your *hope*.

When you realize that, life becomes exhilarating.

This I call to mind
and therefore I have hope:
Because of the LORD's great love we are not consumed,
for his compassions never fail.
They are new every morning;
great is your faithfulness.
LAMENTATIONS 3:21–23

CHAPTER 1

His Faithful Promises

Let us hold unswervingly to the hope we
profess, for he who promised is faithful.

HEBREWS 10:23

For months after my wife, Katrina, moved to her new address in heaven, I was lost in the evenings. We'd always been together or at least spoken several times a night, even when I was traveling. After her passing, I managed the days tolerably but couldn't find an evening routine. I'm not an entertainment fan. Then the Lord whispered to me and said, "*Why don't you become a student again? Remember how you used to hunker over your desk in the dorm or at a study carrel in the library? You still have so much to learn.*"

So, I began devoting a couple of hours in the evening to study, and I enjoyed it very much. Still, there was a terrible gap between my study time and my bedtime, and the devil tried filling it with all kinds of unsettling feelings. Then the Lord whispered to me, *"Why don't you have evening vespers—your own personal evening vespers before retiring?"*

"Lord, I don't even really know what *vespers* means."

"Well, in the mornings you have morning devotions right after you get out of bed. What if you ended each day by singing to or listening to a hymn, reading aloud your current Scripture memory project, and offering the Lord's Prayer? It would be like your own little liturgical ending to the day. Then you could go to bed knowing I was there with you—faithfully."

Now, I didn't have that conversation audibly with the Lord, but that seemed to be what He was saying in the still, small voice with which He counsels us, and it has worked. Even in the face of loss and loneliness, the Lord knows how to reacquaint us with His faithfulness. From the rising of the sun to its setting, God is faithful.

Joseph G. Rainsford was an Irish pastor who, in the 1800s, wrote a book about the faithfulness of God. One chapter was devoted to the core issue of God's commitment to fulfill His promises to us. Calling God *"the* Promiser—par excellence,"[1] Rainsford said that every biblical promise is guaranteed by the cross and secured by the "yea and amen" of the risen Jesus.[2]

The steadfastness of God's promises is built on four great pillars, said Rainsford:

1. God's holiness, which will not allow Him to deceive.
2. God's goodness, which will not allow Him to forget.
3. God's truth, which will not allow Him to change.
4. God's power, which will not allow Him to fail.[3]

God comforts us as a mother comforts, said Rainsford. He pities as a father pities his children. He sympathizes as a friend who sticks closer than a brother. He protects us as a king. He heals us as a physician, and He is as devoted to us as a faithful spouse.[4]

Those concepts permeate Hebrews, a New Testament book written to Jewish Christians facing uncertain times due to rising waves of persecution. Some of these seasoned believers felt like giving up. In chapter 10, the writer used one of the greatest pictures of prayer in the Bible by reminding his readers that they had direct, immediate access into the Most Holy Place—into the very presence of God—through the blood of Christ, our great High Priest (Hebrews 10:19–22). Therefore, he said, we must "hold unswervingly to the hope we profess, for he who promised is faithful" (v. 23).

Whatever you're facing today, remember you have instant, immediate, perpetual access into God's presence through your Great High Priest. God's holiness, His goodness, His truth, and His power are faithfully transmitted to us by virtue of His promises. You can hold them as tightly as a handgrip on a lurching train.

From morning's dawn to evening's vespers, the Lord is faithful.

....

God's promises are a staff for the hand of faith to grasp.

REV. JOSEPH G. RAINSFORD

CHAPTER 2

The Divine Facts

Great is your faithfulness.

LAMENTATIONS 3:23

Many of us can describe the worst day of our lives, when our greatest fears were realized, our nightmares came true, and we almost wished we had died before that day arrived. How hard to bear those times of terrible grief, loss, sorrow, and desolation.

The prophet Jeremiah spent decades preaching to the people of Jerusalem, few of whom listened to him. He warned, instructed, predicted, and wept as he begged people to repent. The culture around him devolved, and revivals no longer occurred. Despite his pleas, he saw few converts. His society went from worse to worst, and judgment fell in 587 BC, when the Babylonian army broke through the walls, slaughtered the people, burned the city, and destroyed God's temple.

It was the most traumatic day of his life.

The Old Testament book of Lamentations is a series of five sorrowful songs—funeral dirges—Jeremiah composed about the horror, and they are among the saddest words ever written. But right in the middle of them, he said, "Yet this I call to mind and therefore I have hope . . ." (Lamentations 3:21).

If you'll pause there a moment, you'll find the secret to resiliency. Even in the middle of Jeremiah's pain, he stopped and reminded himself of the divine facts.

"Yet this I call to mind and therefore I have hope: Because of the Lord's great love we are not consumed, for his compassions never fail. They are new every morning; great is your faithfulness" (vv. 21–23).

God's love is greater than we know. His depths of compassion are limitless. His blessing comes afresh every morning. He doesn't change, and His faithfulness is as great as His unfathomable nature.

Thomas Chisholm was a farmer, publisher, preacher, husband, and father. At age fifty-seven, he studied Lamentations 3 and wrote a poem about it. Someone set it to music, making it a beloved hymn.

Great is Thy faithfulness, O God my Father,
There is no shadow of turning with Thee;
Thou changest not, Thy compassions, they fail not
As Thou hast been Thou forever wilt be.

Great is Thy faithfulness! Great is Thy faithfulness!
Morning by morning new mercies I see;
All I have needed Thy hand hath provided—
Great is Thy faithfulness, Lord, unto me!

Summer and winter, and springtime and harvest,
Sun, moon and stars in their courses above,
Join with all nature in manifold witness
To Thy great faithfulness, mercy and love.

Pardon for sin and a peace that endureth,
Thine own dear presence to cheer and to guide;
Strength for today and bright hope for tomorrow,
Blessings all mine, with ten thousand beside![1]

When you have a hard day—even the hardest—call this to mind and regain hope: God's lordship is so much greater than your hardship. Life may change, but the Lord doesn't. Great is His faithfulness!

....

Calm me, O God, and keep me calm.

THOMAS OBADIAH CHISHOLM

CHAPTER 3

His Faithful Guidance

Send me your light and your faithful care, let them lead me.

PSALM 43:3

Madeline Carroll grew up in Los Angeles, where her mother was a homemaker and her dad a building contractor. As a child, Madeline appeared in plays and commercials, and soon she was showing up in major motion pictures. Her career was headed in the right direction—until she was asked to disrobe. Madeline, a committed Christian, refused, and she found herself turning down role after role on television and in movies because of her standards. Her agent told her it was impossible for her to make it in Hollywood without taking nude roles. Madeline almost took his advice, but she felt God had called her to minister in the film industry, so she didn't give up.

One day she was offered a role she could accept, and then another, and another. Her role in the movie *I Can Only Imagine* was a breakout moment for her. "The biggest thing I can say is, God is so faithful," Madeline told a reporter on the red carpet. "He is so faithful over our dreams . . . Each step I took, the Lord literally just made the path clear before me. He is a faithful Person if you are faithful to Him. He is faithful to you and He has been so faithful to me. He has your dreams; He is a faithful God. He is an all-covering God and He will make a way where there is no way."[1]

God gives us hopes, aspirations, burdens, dreams, and desires. As we grow to know Him better, He refines our inner compass and makes a way for us. Through God-given wisdom and inner convictions, He helps us chart our course. Through circumstances and wise counsel, we can establish our steps. Our jobs, careers, and lives may not unfold as we envision, and some days will feel discouraging. But there's never a time when God doesn't listen to us when we pray the words of Psalm 43:3: *Send me your light and your faithful care, let them lead me.*

He guides us like a shepherd, counsels us like a parent, protects us like an army, and enriches us like a king. Do you need His faithful guidance today? Then adopt Psalm 43:3 as your prayer all day long—"Lord, send me your light and your faithful care to lead me moment by moment and step-by-step."

. . . .

Our faith ebbs and flows, but God's faithfulness, like
a great rock, stands unmoved and immovable.

REV. JOSEPH G. RAINSFORD

CHAPTER 4

Consider Him Faithful

And by faith even Sarah, who was past childbearing age, was enabled to bear children because she considered him faithful who had made the promise.

HEBREWS 11:11

Hebrews 11 is called the "Hall of Faith" of the Bible, because it's a roll call of Old Testament heroes who trusted God, even in impossible situations. The recurring phrase is *"By faith . . ."*

Faith is simply counting on God's faithfulness. In the case of Sarah, God told her and her husband, Abraham, that He would give them a son and multiply their descendants. God had appointed Abraham and Sarah as the progenitors of the nation of Israel, through whom would come the Messiah.

Sarah was one of the most beautiful women in the Bible. She

was so beautiful that Abraham worried someone would kill him and seize her. But as the decades passed, Sarah's beauty faded with old age, and Abraham grew too decrepit to father a child.

Yet God had promised.

Would you believe a child—Isaac—was conceived when Abraham was one hundred and Sarah was ninety?

Sarah had only a single promise, and, though she wasn't always perfect in the exercise of her faith, she reckoned on God's faithfulness and gained the victory. You and I have a Bible filled with promises. Whenever I'm troubled, I go to my desk, open my Bible to where I've left off reading last time, and say, "Lord, is there a promise somewhere in these next chapters for me?"

Then, with an engineer's pencil in hand, I start reading verse after verse, chapter after chapter. When I find the verse God has for me, I underline it with my pencil and then copy it with a pen into my prayer journal. I might also print it on some cards and post them where I can see them.

Recently I've been hanging on to 1 Thessalonians 5:23: "May God himself, the God of peace, sanctify you through and through." When my wife, Katrina, passed away last year, I became a single person again. It's not easy to establish new routines, and I've had moments when I've not done so well.

But the phrase "through and through" has helped me.

The word *sanctify* means, in simple terms, to be set apart

for Jesus, becoming more and more like Him. In this new and unwanted phase of life, I've been praying, "Lord, sanctify me through and through." And by faith, I know He is accomplishing that, even if the progress seems slow.

In your difficult or impossible circumstances, do as Sarah did: consider God faithful, for He can work in any situation—through and through.

. . . .

Faith, mighty faith, the promise sees and looks to that alone;
laughs at impossibilities and cries: It shall be done!

CHARLES WESLEY

CHAPTER 5

"This Is a Miracle"

For the LORD is good and his love endures forever;
his faithfulness continues through all generations.

PSALM 100:5

My friend Leonard DeWitt in a book titled *Jehovah-Jireh Is His Name*, recounted the spiritual struggle he encountered in high school. As a teen, he felt that God wanted him to yield his entire life to Christ, but Leonard wasn't ready to do that. He was clinging to some plans of his own, outside of God's will for him.

"One Sunday, as we were getting ready for Sunday school and church," Leonard wrote, "my mother informed us that she was staying home because my father was ill. When we came home, Dad was worse. We carried him out and put him in my brother's car. They headed for the hospital."

That afternoon Leonard and his younger brother did their chores, but they were anxious about their dad. When their work was done, they walked three miles to the hospital. As they stepped into the hospital corridor, their mother came to them crying. "Your dad had a heart attack. He is in a coma and won't live through the night."

During that terrible evening, Leonard battled intense guilt. "My prodigal heart had caused both my parents considerable pain and grief," he said. "Now it appeared I would never be able to ask Dad's forgiveness. Even worse, he was at death's door and he was not a Christian."

Many people gathered at the family's church that night and prayed for Mr. DeWitt. At the same time, Leonard was engaged in an intense inner battle. Before the sun came up, he had totally and irrevocably offered himself to the Lord Jesus for whatever God wanted.

The next morning, Leonard went to the hospital and was surprised to see his father sitting up in bed and talking to his mother and the examining doctor. "This is a miracle," said the doctor. "I had nothing to do with it. Someone much bigger than me took care of this problem."

"No words could describe the joy that came to our family that day," recalls Leonard. "A compassionate Lord healed my father and gained the victory in my life at the same time."[1]

In time, Leonard's dad also found Jesus Christ as his Savior.

Our faith in God's faithfulness invokes blessings on the generations around us and on all the generations to come.

"For the LORD is good and his love endures forever; his faithfulness continues through all generations."

....

Faith is holding on to the faithfulness of God, and, as long as you do that, you cannot go wrong. Faith does not look at the difficulties . . . Faith does not look at itself . . . Faith looks at God.

MARTYN LLOYD-JONES

CHAPTER 6

HOW WE BECOME FAITHFUL

But the fruit of the Spirit is . . . faithfulness.

GALATIANS 5:22

J esus once compared Himself to a grapevine, and us to the branches. When we stay connected with Him, the sap of the Holy Spirit flows through Him to us, producing fruit, more fruit, and much fruit (John 15:1–8).

The apostle Paul described this fruit, which includes faithfulness, in Galatians 5.

That's why we're commanded to be filled with the Spirit (Ephesians 5:18), which means daily offering our lives to Christ so every cell of our being can be saturated with the Holy Spirit, like a sponge dripping with water. In the process we are "transformed into his image with ever-increasing glory, which comes from the Lord, who is the Spirit" (2 Corinthians 3:18).

What does it look like to be transformed into Christ's image? It's not a matter of looking like Christ physically or dressing in His style of clothing. The verse is talking about absorbing and reflecting His essential personality and core attitudes—His character traits.

According to Galatians 5:22–23, there are nine of them.

First, Jesus is loving, and His love for you and me drove Him to the cross. Greater love has no one than this, that He lay down His life for His friends (John 15:13).

Second, He is joyful. If we could see Him in person, His joy would radiate like sunshine.

Third, He possesses incredible peace of heart and mind. He never has a panic attack, never loses His composure.

Fourth, He is patient and forbearing. He puts up with our faults and failures as He forms us into better people.

Fifth, He is kind. Children loved being lifted into His arms and blessed.

Sixth, He is good—essentially, intrinsically, perpetually good, with no trace of evil or meanness.

Seventh, He is faithful. Every word He speaks is true, trustworthy, genuine, and unfailing.

Eighth, He is gentle. We can often feel His gentle touch on our hearts.

Finally, He is self-controlled. Self-control is the ability to do what we don't feel like doing, and the determination not to do what we do feel like doing, as regulated by the will of God.

This is the fruit of the Spirit. When we're fully yielded to Christ, the Holy Spirit gradually but actively reproduces those nine attitudes within us. We slowly but steadily grow more loving, joyful, peaceful, patient, kind, good, faithful, gentle, and self-controlled as husbands, wives, friends, and workers in His kingdom.

Because Jesus is faithful in every way, then, we become steady, mature, and trustworthy, like Him.

....

The Christian life is a moment-by-moment miracle, lived by the power of the Holy Spirit. The Holy Spirit takes the joy and peace of Christ and reproduces them in and through our lives. He takes the love of Christ and manifests it through us.

ROBERT C. MCQUILKIN

CHAPTER 7

THE MEASURE OF GOD'S FAITHFULNESS

And he passed in front of Moses, proclaiming, "The
LORD, the LORD, the compassionate and gracious God,
slow to anger, abounding in love and faithfulness."

EXODUS 34:6

N otice the word *abounding* in the scripture above. It means
"existing in vast quantities, richly supplied, filled to overflowing." That's the measure of God's faithfulness. He abounds
in faithfulness. It exists in vast quantities, overflowing, richly
supplying all your needs.

In the book of Exodus, Moses descended from Mount Sinai
to learn the Israelites had crafted a golden calf and committed
idolatry and scandal. He was so enraged he threw down the Ten
Commandments—the two stone tablets that had been chiseled by

the finger of God. They broke to pieces at the foot of the mountain (32:19).

Later, the Lord told Moses, "Chisel out two stone tablets like the first ones, and I will write on them the words that were on the first tablet, which you broke" (34:1). Moses did so, and early in the morning he carried the two tablets up Mount Sinai, where God rewrote His commands. Almighty God also proclaimed His great name with these words: "The Lord, the Lord, the compassionate and gracious God, slow to anger, abounding in love and faithfulness, maintaining love to thousands, and forgiving wickedness, rebellion and sin. Yet he does not leave the guilty unpunished" (34:6–7).

This time when Moses came down the mountain with the two tablets of the covenant law in his hands, his face was radiant (34:29).

As you hike through life, what's your appearance? Are you like Moses the first time he walked down the mountain, or the second?

There's a lot to be enraged about nowadays, and righteous indignation is appropriate. But when our faces are grim and our countenances stern, it does little to spread the joy of Christ. Psalm 34:5 says, "Those who look to him are radiant; their faces are never covered with shame."

Psalm 19:8 tells us, "The commands of the Lord are radiant,

giving light to the eyes." When we have the Word of a faithful God moisturizing our minds like an emollient, it changes our complexions. I said in an earlier chapter that when we become more like Christ, it doesn't mean we physically look like Him. But I'm rethinking that. As we mature and mellow with the mind of Christ, the expressions on our faces—the joy, peace, wisdom, and character—must surely be a reflection of the countenance of Christ.

One further thing. What do you call a crowd of radiant people who gather to worship? Ephesians 5:27 would call it "a radiant church, without stain or wrinkle or any other blemish, but holy."

The best cosmetic in the world is the radiance of Christ. He abounds in faithfulness, and we radiate Him. His abundant mercy saves; His abundant faithfulness keeps; His abundant victory reigns.

....

If you are filled with light, with no dark corners, then your whole life
will be radiant, as though a floodlight were filling you with light.

JESUS OF NAZARETH

CHAPTER 8

THIRTY-NINE PROMISES

What if some were unfaithful? Will their unfaithfulness
nullify God's faithfulness? Not at all!

ROMANS 3:3–4

I n Romans 3, the apostle Paul explained the blessings of being Jewish. To the Hebrews God had entrusted His Old Testament Scriptures. Those Scriptures were filled with promises, yet the Jewish people—along with the rest of us—have failed to live as God commanded. Will this nullify God's faithfulness to His promises?

Not at all! He will keep every promise He has made in every Old Testament book.

God will keep His promise . . .

in Genesis 15:1, to be our shield and very great reward.

in Exodus 33:14, to go with us and give us rest.

in Leviticus 26:12, to walk among us and be our God.

in Numbers 6:24–25, to bless us and keep us and make His face shine upon us.

in Deuteronomy 4:7, to be near us when we pray.

in Joshua 1:9, to be with us wherever we go.

in Judges 6:24, to be our peace.

in Ruth 4:15, to renew our lives and sustain us in old age.

in 1 Samuel 2:9, to guard the feet of His faithful servants.

in 2 Samuel 22:29, to turn our darkness into light.

in 1 Kings 3:12, to give us wise and discerning hearts.

in 2 Kings 3:16, to fill our dry valleys with water.

in 1 Chronicles 28:20, to be with us without interruption until our work is done.

in 2 Chronicles 15:7, to reward our labor.

in Ezra 8:22, to rest His gracious hand on those who look to Him.

in Nehemiah 2:20, to give us success in doing His will.

in the book of Esther, to accomplish His providential plans for His people.

in Job 19:26, to resurrect our bodies at the end of time.

in Psalm 34:7, to send His angels to encamp around those who fear Him.

in Proverbs 3:6, to direct the steps of those who acknowledge and trust Him (see KJV).

in Ecclesiastes 2:24–26, to give us satisfaction, enjoyment, and wisdom.

in Song of Songs 2:4, to unfurl His banner of love over us.

in Isaiah 40:31, to renew our strength.

in Jeremiah 23:23, to be a God who is nearby and not far away.

in Lamentations 3:23, to bestow new blessings upon us every morning.

in Ezekiel 36:25, to cleanse us from all our impurities.

in Daniel 4:17, to rule over the course of history (see the NLT).

in Hosea 6:1, to bind up our wounds.

in Joel 2:14, to leave behind a blessing for us.

in Amos 9:15, to restore the nation of Israel to Him in His timing.

in Obadiah v. 21, to prevail in bringing forth His kingdom.

in Jonah 2:7, to hear our prayers as they ascend to His holy temple.

in Micah 4:2, to teach us His ways, that we may walk in His paths.

in Nahum 1:7, to be our refuge in times of trouble.

in Habakkuk 2:14, to one day fill the earth with the knowledge of the glory of the Lord.

in Zephaniah 3:17, to rejoice over us with singing.

in Haggai 2:19, to bless us from this day on.

in Zechariah 2:5, to be a wall of fire around us and the
glory in our midst.

in Malachi 3:10, to honor our support of His work by
opening the windows of heaven and pouring out
blessings we don't have enough room to receive.

Every word God speaks in the Bible is, in some way, directly
or indirectly, a promise, for it gives His thoughts, His mind, His
intentions, and His faithful words to our needy hearts.

....

In such a world as this, where duties perpetually demand our
practice, and difficulties and trials are ever surrounding us, what
can we do better than to treasure up the Promises in our hearts?

ISAAC WATTS

CHAPTER 9

OUT ON A LEDGE

He is the Rock, his works are perfect, and all
his ways are just. A faithful God who does
no wrong, upright and just is he.

DEUTERONOMY 32:4

Clay Engel moved to Colorado to play baseball in the Rocky Mountain Collegiate League. One evening he went hiking in Estes Park, planning to spend the night in his hammock. As he looked for a place to camp in the darkness, he became trapped on a ledge with no way up or down.

"When I realized I was stuck, I had a very overwhelming panic attack," he said, "which I've never experienced before or since. It was very supernatural, like the enemy. There was all this fear and anxiety and panic. It overwhelmed me. I thought so many things, the thoughts were flying through my head. I remember crying out to God saying, 'God, I need help!'"

In his panic, Clay tumbled off the cliff and hit the ground so hard he was unconscious for five hours. He had a fractured skull, a fractured vertebra, and a deep gash through his thigh. When he came to, he had no idea where he was. He staggered to his feet and began limping down the mountain.

Then something mysterious happened. He recalls a short woman with a white shawl walking beside him. The two never spoke. She walked with him to a cabin, and then he saw her no more. A retired Navy medic opened the door, and he instantly went into action, calling the paramedics and saving Clay's life.

Today Clay is married, still involved in baseball, and zealous for serving Jesus Christ.

"I think what I've realized the most and something I've seen very clearly is how faithful God is . . . I've experienced God's faithfulness so clearly."[1]

In Deuteronomy 32, Moses wrote his final sermon for Israel—a closing song. "Oh, praise the greatness of our God!" he sings. "He is the Rock, his works are perfect, and all his ways are just. A faithful God who does no wrong" (v. 3–4).

When you're stuck on a ledge, remember that God is your Rock—and He is faithful.

....

Though I cannot tell the reason, I can trust, and so am blest. /
God is love, and God is faithful. So in perfect peace I rest.

I. G. W., *STREAMS IN THE DESERT*

CHAPTER 10

LIVE IN RELIANCE ON
HIS FAITHFULNESS

*I have always been mindful of your unfailing love
and have lived in reliance on your faithfulness.*

PSALM 26:2–3

Several years ago, Michelle Aguilar Whitehead won the television contest *Biggest Loser* by shedding 110 pounds and gaining a quarter-million dollars in prize winnings. When she returned home after the taping but before the show aired, one of her friends told her, "You know, I never saw you as someone who was overweight. You're just Michelle. I just see you. I don't see anyone else."

To Michelle, that was a great compliment. She told journalist Leah MarieAnn Klett, "A huge lesson weight loss taught me was, we think everyone sees our flaws, but really, they see you. They see who you are as a friend, a wife, a mother, a sister. They see *who* you are and not *what* you are. The scale wants to tell you what you are. It's a great way to check in or keep you accountable, but it's a tool, it doesn't define who you are."

Michelle says that in her physical health and in her roles as wife and mother, she has relied on God's faithfulness every step of the way.

"Trusting God makes all the difference in the world. You are capable of more than you believe. For me, I could not have done 'Biggest Loser' or be the wife and mom I am today without my relationship with Jesus."[1]

In Psalm 26, the psalmist David said, "I have always been mindful of your unfailing love and have lived in reliance on your faithfulness." His confidence wasn't in his own image or impact. It wasn't in his own rule and reign; it wasn't in his health or wealth. All those things could disappear in a moment. He triumphed in life by relying on God's great faithfulness and being mindful of God's unfailing love.

The word *mindful* means to have your "mind full" of something. When we become diligent students of the Bible, we fill our minds with God's truth. We discover His unfailing love. We read about His faithfulness. We find and claim His promises with the absolute security that He will honor them.

Mindfulness is akin to meditation. The Bible tells us to mediate on Scripture day and night (Psalm 1). As I indicated in my book, *Reclaiming the Lost Art of Biblical Meditation*, we should have Scripture flowing through our minds constantly, like water through a pump. We do this by thinking about Bible verses at every opportunity and by singing the classic hymns of the faith. When I awaken in the morning, I've learned to start quoting Scripture before getting out of bed, and to choose a hymn to sing throughout the day. This allows me to stay mindful of His divine reliability.

When the *real* you meets the *real* Christ, it makes a *real* difference!

To His free grace, to His inviolable faithfulness,
and to His unchangeable love, we must ascribe that
we are where we are, and what we are.

REV. JAMES SMITH

CHAPTER 11

GOD'S INK

God is faithful, who has called you into fellowship
with his Son, Jesus Christ our Lord.

1 CORINTHIANS 1:9

During a series of engagements in Southeast Asia, I met a fellow from a Communist nation. His smile was like sunshine, and we became fast friends. Tuan's arm bore a tattoo in Asian letters.[1] The symbols spelled: *PEACE. CLEAN. ETERNAL.* Tuan explained that he'd grown up with haunting emptiness, and these were the three things he had so desperately wanted as a teenager: a sense of peace, a feeling of being clean, and eternal life. A tattoo artist had inked the three symbols onto his arm.

After high school, Tuan traveled to eastern Europe for university studies, and a girl invited him to a Christmas party sponsored by an Asian church. That night, he was reacquainted with Christmas songs he had heard from the American holiday movies he'd watched all his life. But now he heard them in his own language. He understood the words. In this way, he learned the gospel message and met Jesus. His entire life was suddenly emblazed with the words representing the very things he had so deeply desired: *PEACE. CLEAN. ETERNAL.*

Today Tuan is back in his own country, facing persecution but enthusiastically sharing the story of Christmas and of the Christ who has emblazed all history with His love.

In writing to the Corinthians, the apostle Paul opened on a positive note, thanking God for them. He added, "[God] will also keep you firm to the end, so that you will be blameless on the day of our Lord Jesus Christ. God is faithful, who has called you into fellowship with his Son, Jesus Christ our Lord" (1 Corinthians 1:8–9).

The Lord stamps on our hearts *PEACE. CLEAN. ETERNAL,* and the ink is as indelible as the blood of Christ.[2]

....

The Bible tells us of the past acts of God's faithful love that we may be led to set our hope on God, and to feel assured that He who hath helped will help, and that He who hath loved will love unto the end.

THOMAS ERSKINE

CHAPTER 12

"Strange!"

*The Lord is trustworthy in all he promises and
faithful in all he does. The Lord upholds all who fall
and lifts up all who are bowed down. . . . The Lord is
righteous in all his ways and faithful in all he does.*

PSALM 145:13–14, 17

Someone asked Dr. Rowland V. Bingham to name his most
unusual answer to prayer. Bingham, a missionary leader,
told of an opportunity in Nigeria. A piece of property his mission
needed had come on the market at $10,000. This was a massive
amount in the early 1900s, and Bingham was so burdened he
could hardly sleep. The next day he spoke to a large crowd at
a conference, but he didn't feel free to mention the need. After
the service, his host asked if he had any prayer requests, and
Bingham mentioned the project.

"That's fine," said the man. "I will give you $10,000."

That evening, Bingham's heart was so happy that, again, he could hardly sleep:

Suddenly the Lord spoke very quietly to me by His Spirit . . . He made the inquiry: "Why are you so happy?"

"Dear Lord, how wonderful that prayer has been answered so quickly and completely! Ten thousand dollars in one gift, in one night, without the slightest thought on my part that these dear friends could or would make such a gift!"

Then the Lord said, "Do you have the money?"

"No, my Lord, our friend did not have the money in his pocket to give me, but he promised to go to the bank this morning and send it without delay."

Again the Lord spoke, saying, "All you have is his promise?"

"Yes, Lord, but I am sure he will mail that check this morning."

Then the Lord said very quietly to me, "Strange! Yesterday when you were going to the conference you had My promise, but you were not very happy about it. Now you have a man's promise and your heart is filled with joy and confidence!"

Bingham said, "That answer to prayer, and the deep and

searching rebuke from the Lord is quite possibly the most striking answer to prayer I have had; at least, it has been the most instructive."[1]

The Lord is trustworthy in all His promises and faithful in all He does. If we can trust in human words, how much more in His! His faithfulness secures our happiness and holiness.

....

God's faithfulness means that He always does the right thing in every situation. It also means He'll never fail to meet a promise.

DR. CHARLES STANLEY

CHAPTER 13

A Way Out

No temptation has overtaken you except what is common to mankind. And God is faithful; he will not let you be tempted beyond what you can bear. But when you are tempted, he will also provide a way out so that you can endure it.

1 CORINTHIANS 10:13

I n 1 Corinthians 10, the apostle Paul reminded us of the ancient Israelites, who, even after their miraculous deliverance at the Red Sea, made a mess of themselves. "Now these things occurred as examples to keep us from setting our hearts on evil things as they did," Paul wrote (v. 6). And he mentioned four particular sins we must studiously avoid. These are the four great temptations that can befall even veteran followers of Christ.

- We tolerate things that hinder our spiritual growth— that's idolatry (v. 7).
- We tolerate sexual experience outside of marriage—that's immorality (v. 8).
- We test God's patience by our willfulness and selfishness (v. 9).
- We grumble and complain (v. 10).

Verse 11 says, "These things happened to [the Israelites] as examples and were written down as warnings for us, on whom *the culmination of the ages* has come" (emphasis added).

What a phrase! We are living on the edge of history, at the culmination of the ages. In such days, we simply cannot be beset by beguiling sins.

"So, if you think you are standing firm, be careful that you don't fall!" (v. 12).

And then we come to the great thirteenth verse, which opens this chapter of *Great Is Thy Faithfulness*. Every temptation we encounter is faced by others too, but God is faithful. He will not allow us to be overtempted, but will make a way of escape from any temptation so we can endure it.

The original term Paul used here for "a way out" was the word used for a passageway out of a canyon. Sometimes people wandered into a canyon and became trapped. They couldn't find any pathway leading out. But if they looked hard enough, they could find a pathway out of there, a way of escape.

I can tell you what that way of escape is. It's walking close to Jesus along the goat paths that lead out of trying situations. Overcoming temptation isn't so much a matter of what you do but of who you love. It's very hard for the devil to overcome believers who are living in unbroken fellowship with their faithful Lord.

....

Temptation is the tempter looking through the keyhole into the room where you're living. Sin is drawing back the bolt and making it possible for him to enter.

J. WILBUR CHAPMAN

CHAPTER 14

Enough

Be glad, people of Zion, rejoice in the Lord your
God, for he has given you the autumn rains because
he is faithful. He sends you abundant showers.

JOEL 2:23

If you're like me, you fret over having enough—enough time, enough money, enough strength, enough intelligence. But God is totally unbothered by any insufficiency. He is infinitely supplied, and we cannot thank Him enough for that!

English missionary Helen Roseveare wrote, "There is a wonderful truth that God has *enough* to supply all our needs. *Enough* for salvation, *enough* for forgiveness, *enough* to overcome temptations, *enough* to persevere in adversities, *enough* to calm our fears and anxieties. *Enough* grace, *enough* love, *enough* power. His supply is sufficient to meet not only all our needs, but the needs of everyone else in the world now and at all times."[1]

The prophet Joel wrote his small book of Old Testament prophecy during an economic crisis, when waves of locusts had struck ancient Israel, devastating the harvests. Joel told the people to rend their hearts and return to the Lord. "Who knows?" he said. "He may turn and relent and leave behind a blessing" (Joel 2:14).

And so, the Lord did. He restored what the locusts had eaten (Joel 2:25).

We have "locust invasions" in our own lives, when our funds are low, our spirits are devastated, and we gaze around us in despair at our setting. But God is still faithful. He has enough, and He *is* enough. He will restore what the locusts have eaten and pour out His Spirit on His people (2:28).

The people of Zion rejoiced in the Lord, for He gave them the rains and abundant showers needed for the next harvest.

If you read Joel's book closely, you'll notice that he wasn't just writing about the locust invasion of his own day. He was looking into the distant future and writing about the world in the last days and the final invasion of Israel by its enemies before the return of Christ.

I believe we're living in the final phases of the last days, and we never know when a "locust invasion" of some sort will shake our world. But the Lord still sends showers of blessings on His people. He is faithful, and He will bless us abundantly.

When Christ is everything to us, He is enough for us.

. . . .

> Through the ages, our God has had billions of people
> to deal with. Yet there does not stand under heaven's
> cover, or above the stars, or in hell itself a single soul
> who can say that God is not absolutely faithful.
>
> C. H. SPURGEON

CHAPTER 15

In Your Faithfulness

Lord, hear my prayer, listen to my cry for mercy; in your faithfulness and righteousness come to my relief. . . . Teach me to do your will, . . . may your good Spirit lead me.

PSALM 143:1, 10

Often when I study a passage in the Bible, I'll make a list. For example, in reading Psalm 143, a short prayer of twelve verses, I listed fifteen urgent requests David made to God. Looking at such a list, I often circle the item that seems most relevant to me. Today I circled the phrase "Teach me to do your will."

It's been several months since my wife, Katrina, went to heaven, and I've recently felt the need for fresh anointing from God on my life and labor for this new phase of my working in His kingdom. Two passages have come forcibly to mind.

In John 7:38, Jesus said, "Whoever believes in me, as Scripture has said, rivers of living water will flow from within them."

And Revelation 22:1 says, "Then the angel showed me the river of the water of life, as clear as crystal, flowing from the throne of God and of the Lamb."

Now, I believe that second river, the one in heaven, is literal. When I visualize heaven, I imagine the great city described in Revelation 21–22, with the throne of God in its center and the crystal river flowing from beneath it. More about that later.

But there's a spiritual lesson here. Notice that the river flows from beneath the throne. The throne of God is its fountainhead, and the waters flow from beneath the feet of the Enthroned One.

When the Lord Jesus Christ is enthroned in our hearts, the rivers of His Spirit flow from our innermost being, and they provide refreshment to those around us and to a world in need.

When Jesus is truly our Lord, the rivers of blessing flow to others. When He is enthroned, His mercy, power, and efficacy gush forth. When He is at the center of our priorities and passions, nothing can dam up the river of His blessings through us to others.

On the other hand, when He isn't first in our lives, the streams of blessings dry up. For me, this can happen in an instant, and I instantly know it. I say a sharp word, I have a wrong thought, I indulge my appetite too much. Suddenly I feel frustrated with myself, and I have to take a little walk, ask God's forgiveness, and make sure I'm back where I should be beneath His throne and ready to learn and do His will.

So, my prayer today—and you can make it yours too—is this: "LORD, hear my prayer, listen to my cry for mercy; in your faithfulness and righteousness. . . . Teach me to do your will, . . . may your good Spirit lead me" (Psalm 143:1, 10).

. . . .

May we so trust the love of God and the faithfulness of God that we may have courage to say, "Show me Thy way."

JOHN NELSON DARBY

CHAPTER 16

TWENTY-SEVEN PROMISES

The one who calls you is faithful, and he will do it.

1 THESSALONIANS 5:24

A young man texted me today about a benediction I often use at the close of the Sunday services at our church. A benediction is a final blessing on the people, and one of my favorites is 1 Thessalonians 5:23–24: "May God himself, the God of peace, sanctify you through and through. May your whole spirit, soul and body be kept blameless at the coming of our Lord Jesus Christ. The one who calls you is faithful, and he will do it."

As I said earlier, the word *sanctify* means, in simple terms, to make us more and more like Christ. He is faithful, which means He will do it. He'll also keep all the other promises He has made in the twenty-seven books of the New Testament, promises like these:

- to give rest to those who, weary and burdened, come to Him (Matthew 11:28)
- to reward those who give a cup of water to the thirsty in Jesus' name (Mark 9:41)
- to give the Holy Spirit to those who ask Him (Luke 11:13)
- to give us a peace like the world doesn't know (John 14:27)
- to equip us as His witnesses to the world (Acts 1:8)
- to work all things for the good of those who love Him (Romans 8:28)
- to ensure that our labor in the Lord is not in vain (1 Corinthians 15:58)
- to comfort us in all our trouble (2 Corinthians 1:4)
- to rescue us from this present evil age (Galatians 1:4)
- to do for us immeasurably more than all we ask or imagine (Ephesians 3:20)
- to continue the good work He has begun in us (Philippians 1:6)
- to arrange for us to appear with Christ in glory (Colossians 3:4)
- to give us peace at all times and in every way (2 Thessalonians 3:16)
- to bring Jesus back to earth in His own time (1 Timothy 6:15)
- to guard what we have entrusted to Him (2 Timothy 1:12).

- to help us say no to ungodliness and worldly passions (Titus 2:12)
- to make our partnership with others in the faith effective (Philemon v. 6)
- to produce in us what is pleasing to Him (Hebrews 13:21)
- to use difficulties to give us perseverance and maturity (James 1:3–4)
- to care for all the anxieties we cast on Him (1 Peter 5:7)
- to provide everything we need for a godly life (2 Peter 1:3)
- to forgive all our confessed sin (1 John 1:9)
- to place His truth within us (2 John v. 2)
- to bless us in body and soul (3 John v. 2)
- to keep us from stumbling (Jude v. 24)
- and finally, Jesus promises, "Yes, I am coming soon" (Revelation 22:20).

God's Word is a treasure trove of truth, and His truth includes His promises—from Genesis to Malachi, and from Matthew to Revelation. I've written a short prayer in my journal that says, "Lord, help me to worship and not wallow; to praise and not pout; and not to flounder, but to walk by faith."

....

God never made a promise that was too good to be true.

D. L. MOODY

CHAPTER 17

THE DIGNITY OF HUMILITY

*Not to us, LORD, not to us but to your name be the
glory, because of your love and faithfulness.*

PSALM 115:1

It's amazing how we crave glory and fame. We secretly want to
impress others, and we enjoy knowing when we've impressed
them. I'm as guilty as anyone, and the motivations within me are
the part of me I trust the least. Recently I've been asking myself
afresh, "Why am I doing what I'm doing? Is it really for the Lord,
or is it mostly for me?"

Psalm 115:1 is a good prayer for us to offer: "Not to us, LORD,
not to us but to your name be the glory."

A couple of Sundays ago, I preached from Philippians 2:2–3,
where Paul wrote, "Make my joy complete by being like-minded,
having the same love, being one in spirit and of one mind. Do

nothing out of selfish ambition or vain conceit. Rather, in humility value others above yourselves."

How surprising! The great apostle Paul admitted that his joy was incomplete. It was missing something. It wasn't as full and fulfilling as it should be. His joy was diminished by the divisions within the Philippian church. He asked them to work out their differences and to be humble toward one another so that his joy would be complete.

Division diminishes our joy. When our marriages, homes, friendships, churches, or nations are divided, it lessens our happiness and sense of well-being. When our relationships and those around us are harmonious and happy, it makes our joy complete.

This involves humility, doing nothing out of selfish ambition and vain conceit. Perhaps you need a humbler attitude toward your spouse, your parents, or your associates at work. There is a dignity to humility. Little is gained by being stubborn or acting rudely. In fact, those attitudes—common in our world—are marks of immaturity.

Catherine Graham, longtime publisher of the *Washington Post*, was asked, "Mrs. Graham, you have hosted all the great leaders around the world. What is the single most important trait of all great leaders?"

Instantly she replied, "The absence of arrogance."[1]

I recall hearing the late Billy Graham once say that he had to be very careful about the publicity and recognition attached to his ministry, for God had told him, "I am the LORD; that is my name! I will not yield my glory to another" (Isaiah 42:8).

And why should the Lord receive every ounce of the glory? Because of His love and faithfulness. He has many other qualities, of course, and all of them worthy of praise. But in Psalm 115:1, the writer was caught up in the wonder of God's love and faithfulness, and he gloried God with all his heart.

Take a moment to offer the same prayer aloud: "Not to us, LORD, not to us, but to your name be the glory, because of your love and faithfulness."

....

To trust in ourselves is to build upon quick sands; but the truth
of God is a golden pillar for faith . . . He abideth faithful.

THOMAS WATSON

CHAPTER 18

THE SHORTEST CHAPTER
IN THE BIBLE

*Praise the LORD, all you nations; extol him, all you
peoples. For great is his love toward us, and the faithfulness
of the LORD endures forever. Praise the LORD.*

PSALM 117

The writer of Psalm 117 had a broad audience. He was
preaching to "all you nations" and "all you peoples"—to
everyone on earth. He believed that every single person has
grounds to extol God for His great love toward us and His ever-
enduring faithfulness. I'm one of the 7.8 billion people currently
on earth, so this passage is addressed to me and to you. It's also
for our children. How vital for our youngsters to learn about
God's faithfulness from infancy.

I recently read a blog by homeschool mother Julie H. Lake, who recalled some scenes from her childhood:

> I remember sitting on the floor in Ms. Sammie Lou's Sunday school class and watching as she made the Bible come to life right before my eyes. Fuzzy felt disciples and Jesus all clinging to the fuzzy felt board. There was also Noah, Moses, Daniel, Queen Esther, and many others. I was introduced to all of them. And I believed. It didn't occur to me not to believe.
>
> In Vacation Bible School, in the middle of cookies and punch, glitter and glue and games of Red Rover, there were the familiar choruses of "He's Got the Whole World in His Hands" and "Jesus Loves the Little Children." We took turns reading from the Bible, and I heard about God's faithfulness over and over again. And still, it didn't occur to me not to believe and take Jesus at His Word.
>
> As a teenager, I made my way to the altar during a youth revival and publicly professed Christ as my Savior. My relationship with Him began sweetly and tenderly, full of hope and promise. He has remained faithful to me all these years. I wish I could say the same about me. But I am fearful when I should be faithful, impatient when I should be patient and profoundly ill-tempered when love is the better choice.

She continued, "In the midst of global chaos, I need to be reminded more than ever that God does, indeed, have the whole world in His hands."[1]

We're all growing. We're not what we once were, nor yet what we shall be. But memorizing this short psalm will help. If you teach it to your children, they can tell their friends they've memorized a whole chapter of the Bible. Let's pass God's faithfulness down to our youngsters.

Psalm 117 is the shortest chapter in the Bible, but it has a message deeper than the seas and higher than the heavens. We're to praise the Lord without ceasing because His love is great and His faithfulness is eternal.

Praise the Lord!

In these times of such uncertainty, God is constant and reliable. He is present. He is faithful. He is approachable. Whether you find him in a church building, on your knees at your bedside, or on a fuzzy board, just know. He's got this whole chaotic world firmly in His hands, and He loves us. He loves us so very much. He even has the scars to prove it.

JULIE LAKE, HOMESCHOOLING MOTHER AND BLOGGER

CHAPTER 19

A GIGANTIC ARCHWAY

For this reason he had to be made like them, fully human in every way, in order that he might become a merciful and faithful high priest in service to God, and that he might make atonement for the sins of the people.

HEBREWS 2:17

One day long ago, God Himself rose from the highest throne in heaven as the angelic hosts looked on in stunned silence. He stepped over the banister of heaven and dove into world history through the womb of Mary, a young lady who had been overshadowed by the Holy Spirit in a dusty town in ancient Israel.

We'll never fully understand it, but the mystery of it makes us marvel. The Infinite became an infant!

According to Hebrews 1:8, Jesus Christ is and always will be

God Almighty, the second person of the Trinity. God the Father said to Him, "Your throne, O God, will last for ever and ever." But in Hebrews 2, we're told that Jesus Christ also became human—a man—and entered the family of humanity. "Since the children [all of us] have flesh and blood, he too shared in their humanity so that by his death he might break the power of him who holds the power of death—that is, the devil—and free those who all their lives were held in slavery by their fear of death" (vv. 14–15).

Verse 17 says, "For this reason he had to be made like them, fully human in every way."

Fully God, yet fully human in every way!

The God-man!

Many people don't really understand this about Jesus Christ. He was and is and always will be divine—that is, God. But when the Holy Spirit overshadowed the virgin Mary, somehow, through a miracle of conception, Jesus Christ also assumed a human nature. He didn't leave behind His human nature when He returned to heaven. He is and always will be both God and Man. When we see Him in heaven, we'll see a human being, yet we'll also see God, both natures woven into one personality.

Why?

So that He could become a merciful and faithful high priest in service of God and that He might make atonement for the sins of the people.

As your great High Priest, Jesus was faithful to love you, to shed His blood for you, to bring you into a relationship with Him, and to give you eternal life. He's also faithful to watch over all your steps, pray over all your needs, carry all your burdens, and turn all things for good in your life.

Oh, how He loves you and me!

....

The faithfulness of God is like a gigantic archway, spanning human history from its beginning to its ending.

J. SIDLOW BAXTER

CHAPTER 20

"In All He Does"

*Sing to him a new song; play skillfully, and
shout for joy. For the word of the LORD is right
and true; he is faithful in all he does.*

PSALM 33:3–4

Jordan St. Cyr, a Christian singer/songwriter in Canada, and
his wife, Heather, recently learned their newborn daughter
has Sturge–Weber syndrome, which affects her brain devel-
opment and causes a port-wine stain on her face. In a recent
interview, Jordan spoke of how traumatic it's been but how
wonderfully God has been with them. It's helped them rediscover
Jesus in a whole new way, he said. "It sounds so cliché, but when
we get to the end of ourselves, God is so faithful."[1]

Out of those lessons, Jordan is creating new songs of praise.

In reading Jordan's story, I couldn't help thinking of Psalm

33. The writer started creating new songs when he realized afresh that God "is faithful in all he does."

"Sing joyfully to the LORD, you righteous," he wrote. "It is fitting for the upright to praise him. Praise the LORD with the harp; make music to him on the ten-stringed lyre. Sing to him a new song; play skillfully, and shout for joy" (vv. 1–3).

And why should we sing joyfully and play skillfully?

Because God is faithful in all He does (v. 4).

He isn't faithful in *some* of what He does, or in *most* of what He does, but in *all* He does. Unfaithful, unreliable, and undependable—these can never be modifying adjectives for our God and His faithfulness. His total faithfulness calls for total trust from us, and it results in total praise. His steadiness fuels our songs, and His perfections prompt our praise.

We often rediscover His faithfulness when the burdens of life drive us afresh to Him and into His Word. The Lord never wastes our trials. Somehow our fears and infirmities become the fertilizer of the soul, enriching us and enabling us to grow to new heights.

Notice one more thing about Psalm 33:3. The writer tells us to sing a new song to God. I love the great hymns, which we must never lose. I'm also excited about modern praise and worship music. In both the classic and the contemporary, learn to pay attention to the lyrics. Look for songs that are objective, not just subjective. An objective song focuses on God and His attributes (such as the hymn, "O Worship the King" or the praise songs "Indescribable," "Blessed be the Name" and "Awesome God"). A subjective song is largely about us, our rescue from sin and shame; our chains are broken; our freedom; our needs; our fears; our purpose. We need both kinds of songs, but too many subjective songs create narcissistic worshippers. A healthy dose of objective music centers our attention of God and His endless attributes—like His faithfulness. The older I get, the more I want to sing of the Lord, and the less I want to focus on myself.

Great faithfulness from God should lead to great thankfulness from us.

....

Oh! beloved friends, if there is a living God, faithful and true, let us hold His faithfulness. . . . Holding His faithfulness, we may face with calm and sober but confident assurance of victory every difficulty and danger; we may count on grace for the work. . . . Let us not give Him a partial trust, but daily, hourly serving Him, holding to God's faithfulness.

J. HUDSON TAYLOR

CHAPTER 21

CHRIST'S FAITHFULNESS
IN LITTLE THINGS

*Righteousness will be his belt and faithfulness
the sash around his waist.*

ISAIAH 11:5

The other day, as I loaded the washing machine, I looked out the window and saw an animal behind my house. I thought it was a fox. I grabbed a pair of World War II army surplus binoculars from the shelf and studied the creature more closely. It was a fawn.

Today I saw what I thought was a large rabbit down in the field. I should have known. The binoculars told me it was my little fawn nestled in the grass.

Binoculars make distant things clear.

The prophet Isaiah had a set of divine binoculars that allowed him to see the distant future, and he wrote clearly about the coming Messiah. We call his book the "Fifth Gospel." Though Isaiah lived seven hundred years before Christ, I could teach every aspect of the birth, life, personality, ministry, death, resurrection, return, and kingdom of Christ without ever leaving Isaiah's sixty-six chapters.

In Isaiah 11, he foresaw that the Messiah would be anointed by the Holy Spirit, who would give Him wisdom, understanding, counsel, might, knowledge, and godly fear. The Messiah would make perfect judgments, be compassionate toward the needy, destroy evil, and ultimately bring peace to earth.

Faithfulness, said Isaiah, would be like a sash around the Lord's waist. He would be girded, enclosed, surrounded, and encircled with faithfulness.

Scottish theologian Sinclair B. Ferguson wrote that in Christ's kingdom, those who are faithful in little are also faithful in much (Luke 16:10). He further observed that Jesus practiced what He preached: He was faithful in honoring His father and mother; He was faithful in living by every word proceeding from the mouth of God; He was faithful to speak graciously and to correct gently; He was faithful to care for those with needs.[1]

The Bible itself is like a pair of binoculars that lets us see Jesus up close. As we read it daily, we're drawn near and we notice that Jesus was Himself faithful to all the Bible taught. He was faithful to meditate on all His Father had written in the Old Testament. He was faithful in biblical meditation and prayer.

Since He is faithful in the details, He can be trusted in the disasters. Since He was faithful in every small thing, He can be trusted with every big issue.

He will be faithful to you in all the concerns of life, whether little or large.

Our Lord's faithfulness in little things, then, was simply a reflection of the perfect beauty He saw in the face of His Father as He listened eagerly to what He had to say.

SINCLAIR B. FERGUSON

CHAPTER 22

HE MAKES NO MISTAKES

I know, LORD, that your laws are righteous, and
that in faithfulness you have afflicted me.

PSALM 119:75

I n 1932, when Rev. A. M. Overton was pastor of a church in Baldwyn, Mississippi, his wife died during childbirth. The newborn also passed away, leaving Pastor Overton with three small children.

During the funeral, the officiating minister saw Reverend Overton scribbling something onto a piece of paper. After the service, he asked Overton about it. The bereaved man handed him the poem he had just written. It said:

> My Father's way may twist and turn
> My heart may throb and ache,

But in my soul I'm glad to know,

He maketh no mistake.

My cherished plans may go astray,

My hopes may fade away,

But still I'll trust my Lord to lead,

For He doth know the way.

There's so much now I cannot see,

My eyesight's far too dim,

But come what may,

I'll simply trust and leave it all to Him.[1]

Psalm 119 is the longest chapter in the Bible, and it emphasizes the wonder of the Word of God. In verse 75, the writer said, in effect, "Lord, I know that every word You speak and everything You do is right. You make no mistakes. So, if I'm having trouble right now, I know You will faithfully use it for my growth and for my good."

God is too wise to be wrong and too faithful to be false. Those who "simply trust and leave it all to Him" will find beneath them the everlasting arms.

We all have to process the challenges that come to us, but when we process them with faith, not with fear, we come to the same conclusion as the psalmist: "In faithfulness you have afflicted me" (Psalm 119:75).

When I look back over the decades, it's clear my greatest

periods of emotional and spiritual growth occurred during times of difficulty. I don't want to go through the trials again, but I'll never forget the lessons I learned at the time. Ruth Bell Graham once told me, "When the devil attacks us, he often goes too far and drives us deeper into our relationship with the Lord." Our Savior faithfully redeems every problem, turns it inside out, and converts it (over time) into a treasure.

There are times when all of us feel that the burden of the cares of life is too heavy for us to bear. There are things about our lives that we cannot control. There is one answer to our dilemma, and that is to rest in and rejoice in God's faithfulness.

DR. JAMES P. GILLS

CHAPTER 23

FEED ON HIS FAITHFULNESS

Dwell in the land, and feed on His faithfulness.

PSALM 37:3 NKJV

P salm 37 was written to Jewish settlers who had moved into newly acquired lands during David's expansion of the kingdom of Israel. The Lord had promised to give Israel all the land from the Mediterranean Sea to the Euphrates River (Joshua 1:4), but the Israelites had possessed only a portion of the allotted territory. David pushed Israel's boundaries outward, and Jewish citizens settled down in the newly occupied regions.

Sometimes God sends us into new and unfamiliar circumstances. We want to make advancements in life and experience all God has for us. But it's no easy task.

David wrote Psalm 37 as an instruction manual. I've been encouraged by the eight instructions found at the beginning of this psalm. Why not open your Bible to this passage and treat the opening verses as a personal Bible study?

Here are God's eight instructions about the onward transitions of life (from the New King James Version).

1. *"Do not fret"* (v. 1). New experiences can bring anxiety, but David tells us three times in this psalm to cast off fretting (vv. 1, 7, 8). If you're prone to worry (as I am), then the next instructions tell us how to minimize fretting.

2. *"Trust in the LORD"* (v. 3). Trust is the mental determination to emphasize God's promises, as great as they are, over our problems, as great as they seem.

3. *"Do good"* (v. 3). When we trust the Lord with our fears, we take the focus off our obsessions and get busy serving Him with the next thing we can find to do.

4. *"Feed on His faithfulness"* (v. 3). To feed on something is to devour it, to chew it up, to swallow it, to get it inside of you, to digest it, to fill yourself with it, to internalize it. Our mental and spiritual diet should be rich in material about the person of God and His infinite faithfulness.

5. *"Delight yourself . . . in the LORD"* (v. 4). To delight in something means we experience a high degree of pleasure or enjoyment in it. This verse says if we delight ourselves in the Lord, He will give us the desires we should have in our

hearts. He will take His desires for us and make them our own—desires that He Himself will fulfill.

6. *"Commit your way to the LORD"* (v. 5). The word *commit* means to totally entrust something valuable into the care and keeping of another, who will take care of it for you. You can commit anything to Him—your opportunities, your plans, your children, your burdens, your future, your day, your difficulties, your dreams.

7. *"Rest in the LORD, and wait patiently for Him"* (v. 7). The word *rest* implies a relaxation of our nerves. And when we want Him to work in some area of life and He doesn't, we have to trust that He will do exactly what's best exactly *when* it's best. The interval between our *wanting* and His *working* is called *waiting*—and that's where faith is built.

8. *"Do not fret"* (v. 7). And so we come full circle. This is the cycle of peace, spinning around God's faithful nature and going before us into lands still to be possessed. You're being carried into the next phases of life by the foot soldiers of God's promises, and not one of them will ever stumble.

So "do not fret—it only causes harm" (v. 8 NKJV).

P.S. Throughout my writings, I've encouraged people to memorize Scripture. Psalm 37:1-8 was my memory project for several months last year, and I'm still going back and reinforcing it. To memorize a passage, start with the first verse and say it aloud. I walk around the room and read it as though preaching: "Do not fret because of evildoers." I might repeat it twenty times. The next day I'll do the same, usually at the end of my daily devotions. Soon it starts to get into my mind; and if I'm watching the news and become agitated by some group causing trouble, I say aloud: "Do not fret because of evildoers." When I have the first phrase halfway learned, I add the next: "Nor be envious of the workers of iniquity." It took me a few months, but now I can close my eyes and quote Psalm 37:1-8, which has worked wonders on my nerves.

Far above all finite comprehension is the unchanging faithfulness of God. Everything about God is great, vast, incomparable. He never forgets, never fails, never falters, never forfeits His Word.

A. W. PINK

CHAPTER 24

"I Am So Happy"

*But the Lord is faithful, and he will strengthen
you and protect you from the evil one.*

2 THESSALONIANS 3:3

Don Hinkle is a journalist and political commentator who lost his dear wife, Bernadette, to a brain tumor. In the months and years since, he's coped with his loss by leaning on 2 Thessalonians 3:3 and the faithfulness of God. In his column, "A Personal Testimony of God's Faithfulness," Don mentioned two examples of this. The first had to do with Bernadette's wedding ring. A few weeks before her tumor was discovered, she was sitting in the living room, playing with the dog, when Don realized she wasn't wearing her wedding ring. He asked her about it, but a phone call interrupted her answer.

A few weeks later, she was gone, and Don had no idea where

to find the ring, and that grieved his heart. He searched every nook and cranny for ten months, then gave up.

One evening, while looking through a drawer in a nightstand, he found it. Evidently Bernadette's finger had swollen, forcing her to remove the ring.

"I am so happy I found it because it reminded me how God brought us together," he said.

The second example of God's faithfulness came through Bernadette's Bible. For over a year, Don didn't touch it. It sat on her chest of drawers, undisturbed. But one day, God gave Don the strength to open it. Inside he found a program for a special service in which he had participated. But the richest blessings came from the notes and verses his wife had jotted in the margins.

"All of this reminds me of God's grace and faithfulness," wrote Don. "I rest in the words of 2 Thessalonians 3:3–5 (KJV): 'But the Lord is faithful, who shall stablish you, and keep you from evil. And we have confidence in the Lord touching you, that ye both do and will do the things which we command you. And the Lord direct your hearts into the love of God, and into the patient waiting for Christ.'"

If we're looking for them, we'll find ongoing tokens of the faithfulness of God in ways that seem small yet are significant to our hearts. The Living Bible (TLB) renders 2 Thessalonians 3:3, "But the Lord is faithful; he will make you strong and guard you from satanic attacks of every kind."

How we need that today—and every day!

Spiritual warfare is real, intense, constant, mysterious and dangerous. We have real enemies in the spiritual realms, but Satan can never overturn God's promises or outwit God's purposes. The Lord is faithful to strengthen us and to protect us from the wiles of Satan. Whatever is happening to you today, lean on 2 Thessalonians 3:3 and the truth it imparts.

When we are most assaulted, we shall be most assisted.

THOMAS WATSON

CHAPTER 25

"One Found Oneself Steadied"

Your word, LORD, is eternal; it stands firm in the
heavens. Your faithfulness continues through all
generations; you established the earth, and it endures.

PSALM 119:89–90

Marie Monson, a Norwegian missionary in China, wrote a true story titled "For Ever, O Lord, Thy Word Is Settled in Heaven," in which she recalled venturing into a dangerous area to lead a Bible study. Suddenly things became unsettled. A retreating army that was killing everyone it met, even women and children, would reach Marie's village the next day.

That evening Marie repeated God's promises in bed, praised Him, and rested unafraid. The next morning the soldier-bandits entered the town. Marie quickly gathered the little group of Chinese Christians in the open courtyard of the house she was using.

"Suddenly the butt-end of a gun battered the gate. I ran and opened it to a solitary soldier, let him in and closed and barred the gate. He was obviously astonished at the unusual scene—a whole group of people calmly standing there, apparently unafraid, although they heard the noise from the streets all around."

Marie invited him to have a cup of tea. He was hungry, so they gave him food. He asked who they were, and they told him about Jesus, who had come with peace and salvation. It was the first time he had heard the name Jesus, but it had an effect on him. Presently he slipped from the house, and no one else bothered Marie and the other villagers. The next day the soldiers were gone.

Marie said, "They left a harried town behind them and in it a little group that believed the Word of the Lord and found Him faithful to His promises toward all who put their trust in Him." Then she added her own lesson: "It was unutterably marvelous to experience over and over again the peace Jesus spoke of, which the world cannot give. In the midst of confusion and distress one found oneself so steadied by such wonderful restfulness of mind that one did not recognize oneself."[1]

Marie Monson has a number of such stories, and some of her writings have helped me at times when my faith needed a shot in the arm. If God is as faithful as He says, we should be more peaceful than we are. And He *is* as faithful as He says, because His Word is settled and established forever in the heavens.

Forever settled in the heavens,

Thy Word, O Lord, shall firmly stand;

Thy faithfulness shall never fail;

The earth abides at Thy command.

PSALM 119:89–90 FROM THE 1912 PSALTER

OF THE UNITED PRESBYTERIAN CHURCH

CHAPTER 26

A Bleak Christmas

This is what the Lord Almighty says: "I will save my people
from the countries of the east and the west. I will bring
them back to live in Jerusalem; they will be my people, and
I will be faithful and righteous to them as their God."

ZECHARIAH 8:7–8

I n the prophet Zechariah's day, the Jewish people were dis-
couraged because most of them were still exiled in Babylon.
Even the Jews back in Jerusalem were struggling with opposition
and lethargy. But God called them to faithfulness, for He Himself
is faithful and righteous. He told them His plan for them didn't
depend on their capability but on His vast ability.

I've found the same is true today.

Recently I was looking at some of my old journal entries, and
I found this one:

December 9, 1986. 4:30 a.m.—I'm sitting here in the living room looking at the Christmas tree, trying to fend off the worry and fear that robbed me of sleep. Across the parking lot sits our new church building, unfinished and further delayed. After seven years here, I feel tired. We've pushed hard, tripled our attendance, constructed a beautiful building, but now there are so many feelings and emotions in me, most of them not good. Resentment. Hurt. Disappointment. Fear. Finally, a sense of failure. I feel I should have done so much more to grow and build up this church. I have real pain in my chest.

O Lord, You who will never leave me or forsake me, You who have loved me with an everlasting love, please stoop to help and deliver Your poor, sin-riddled, helpless, little-faithed servant. I will Thy will. I lay this writing before you as Hezekiah spread out the letter of Sennacherib. O Lord, do not let me dishonor You with unbelief. For Your name's sake, give me victory. If I fail to trust You with these burdens, if I let the reactions of my human nature prevail, it will be dishonoring to You before all the people. And, Lord, I can't hide my feelings; they show up in my eyes. They are published by my face. They are heard in the tone of my voice.

Lord, this all hurts so badly. Somehow I know that it's hurting me more than it should and it's because, I suppose, every pain is amplified by my sinful nature and the devil is trying to wrestle me away from You, at least in the sense of victory in my life.

Endow me with a special dispensation of wisdom, grace, and peace. Give me more faith—and more and more again. And use me! Let a double portion of your Spirit rest upon me. Baptize me with a powerful anointing of Your Holy Spirit. And help, oh, help me. For Your glory. For Jesus' sake and in His name. Amen.

That was thirty-six years ago, and I now see how God was using the pressures to teach me to pray, to persevere, and to let Him regulate my attitudes and emotions by His Spirit. He has blessed and used me, though I'm still so very imperfect. But Jesus counters my imperfection with His resurrection.

And He has been faithful and righteous to me.

To you too!

....

I know of nothing which so stimulates my faith in my Heavenly Father as to look back and reflect on His faithfulness to me in every crisis and every chilling circumstance of life.

W. PHILLIP KELLER

CHAPTER 27

SHELTERED BY GOD'S PROMISES

*But as surely as God is faithful, our message to you
is not "Yes" and "No." For the Son of God, Jesus
Christ, who was preached among you by us—
by me and Silas and Timothy—was not "Yes" and
"No," but in him it has always been "Yes."*

2 CORINTHIANS 1:18–19

T he scripture that opens this chapter holds one of the Bible's
greatest affirmations of God's faithfulness to us, as vested
in His promises. The context is interesting. The apostle Paul had
planned to visit Corinth, but his plans shifted a bit. Some of his
critics in the Corinthian church had claimed he was fickle and
unfaithful. Paul bristled at that, and he told them he was not
undependable. His very message was based on the dependability
of Jesus Christ—God's great "Yes" to us.

Then comes verse 20: "For no matter how many promises God has made, they are 'Yes' in Christ. And so through him the 'Amen' is spoken by us to the glory of God."

Analyze that! God has made many promises. Jesus says, "Yes" to them all. And we say, "Amen!"

Perhaps a couple of examples will be helpful.

- God said, "In all things God works for the good of those who love him" (Romans 8:28). Jesus said, "Yes," and we say, "Amen!"
- God said, "Your strength will equal your days" (Deuteronomy 33:25). Jesus said, "Yes," and we say, "Amen!"

In her book *The Shelter of God's Promises*, contemporary Christian singer Sheila Walsh told of receiving a letter in the mailbox from a woman who wrote about the struggles she had endured—illness, financial hardship, and the breakup of her marriage. Then she said, "I would not have made it this far without the promises of God."[1]

That sentence deeply impressed Sheila and prompted her to conduct her own study of the Bible's promises. "There is the shelter of all God's promises," wrote Sheila. "God not only keeps His promises, but longs to keep them."[2] She continued:

Why would God want to keep us and His promises to us when we mess up so badly?

The Bible reminds us of a truth we often forget, a truth that shines as clear as sunlight: *because God cannot help Himself.* The force of His righteousness and mercy, which were from everlasting and formed the covenant with us, are the unchanging foundation upon which His promises are built. God does not change, nor do the glories of His person and the salvation He engineered for us. God's promises are as dependable as He is.[3]

Many times when I could have gone insane from worry, I was at peace because my soul believed the truth of God's promises. God's Word, together with the whole character of God, as He has revealed Himself, settles all questions.

GEORGE MÜLLER

CHAPTER 28

THE HAIRS OF YOUR HEAD

*I speak of your faithfulness and your saving help. I do not
conceal your love and your faithfulness from the great
assembly. Do not withhold your mercy from me, LORD;
may your love and faithfulness always protect me.*

PSALM 40:10–11

P salm 40 was penned by David, who praised God for lifting
him out of the mud and mire, setting his feet on a rock, and
giving him a song of praise (vv. 1–3). God had delivered David
from a difficult situation, and in return David rededicated himself to the Lord, saying, "I desire to do your will, my God" (v. 8).

He continued, "I speak of your faithfulness . . . I do not conceal . . . your faithfulness . . . May your love and faithfulness
always protect me" (vv. 10–11).

In the next verse, David admitted that he himself had not

been as faithful as he should, saying, "My sins have overtaken me, and I cannot see. They are more than the hairs of my head, and my heart fails within me" (v. 12). Desperate, he cried out, "Be pleased to save me, LORD; come quickly, LORD, to help me" (v. 13).

As David imagined a way to confess his many sins to God, he thought of his own scalp. Apparently, he had a full head of hair, because he imagined every single strand representing a different sin. Have you ever thought of your failures like that? Not everyone has a full head of hair, of course, but the point is well taken. David was saying, in effect, "You might as well try to count the hairs on my head as to count all the sins I need to confess to you."

But God was faithful to forgive every one of them.

Later the Lord Jesus used this same analogy in another way—to reassure us of the faithful care of our heavenly Father: "Are not five sparrows sold for two copper coins? And not one of them is forgotten before God. But the very hairs of your head are all numbered. Do not fear therefore; you are of more value than many sparrows" (Luke 12:6–7 NKJV).

The same God who forgives our sins knows all about us— and He is faithful to lift us from the mud and mire, to set our feet on a rock, and to put a new song in our mouths—a song of praise to our God! That's why we *speak* of His faithfulness, never *conceal* His faithfulness, and *pray* with the assurance that His faithfulness will protect us.

Lord, some days I'm so aware of my shortcomings they seem as many as the hairs on my head. Other days, I'm equally aware of my problems and concerns. The former fills me with regret and guilt; the latter with worry and anxiety. Teach me instead to worship You from the top of my head to the bottom of my feet. You are all mystery and all marvel, and it's marvelous to me! You are precious in my sight because I was first precious in Yours.

You are so precious that the least portion of you is precious; the King keeps a register of every part of you, "The very hairs of your head are all numbered."

C. H. SPURGEON

CHAPTER 29

THE BOOK IN THE GRASS

*LORD, you are my God; I will exalt you and praise
your name, for in perfect faithfulness you have done
wonderful things, things planned long ago.*

ISAIAH 25:1

In his book *Jesus, Our Man in Glory*, A. W. Tozer spoke of how God providentially orders our lives in advance. The same One who has appointed the times and seasons for the nations also knows all the details of our lives in advance.

Tozer said that after becoming a Christian in his youth, he attended a church that seemed to be of little spiritual help to him. One Sunday he awoke in a bad mood and decided, "I'm not going to church today." Instead he went for a walk in the country.

"I turned aside to walk through a grassy field," he said. "In the middle of the field my foot suddenly kicked something hidden in the grass—something red. I stooped and picked up an old red-bound book. It looked as if it had been out in the rain, had dried out, had been rained on again and again and dried out again. The book was not some old literary classic. It was not a discarded book of cheap fiction. It was a Christian handbook: a thousand questions and answers for anyone interested in Bible study."

Tozer opened the book and scanned a few pages. He realized how much he didn't know about the Bible, and how he had discarded the one place where the answers were to be found. He started for home, resolved to be faithful to the One who had providentially planted that book in his pathway.

"In the providence of God it was that day the reminder I needed of the goodness and faithfulness of God," he wrote.[1]

I earnestly believe God knows—yes, has arranged—the details of human history in advance. The prophecies of Scripture explain the events connected with the end of the ages and the return of Christ, and I relish the study of them.

In the same way, I believe God knows—yes, has arranged—the details of the lives of His children. And as we look back on life, we can see we have traveled an appointed way, for the steps of God's people are ordered by Him. In perfect faithfulness, He does good things for us, wonderful things planned long ago.

Trust Him with today's details and with tomorrow's decisions.

The steps of God's people are ordered and orchestrated by the Lord. We plan our ways as best we can, but God directs our footsteps. We make our plans, and He fulfills His purposes in us. The yielded believer is like a child's boat ride at a theme park. We may steer it a little from side by side, but beneath the water are guardrails of godliness that keep us on the right track, at the right speed, and going in the right direction. How important to enjoy the journey with childlike faith!

....

God's total faithfulness is a vibrant, positive message . . . I have come to believe that all the promises of God have been made to assure us weak and changeable humans of God's never-ending goodwill and concern. What God is today He will be tomorrow. And all that God does will always be in accord with all that God is.

A. W. TOZER

CHAPTER 30

THE SAINT'S HIDING PLACE

*I will bow down toward your holy temple and will praise
your name for your unfailing love and your faithfulness.*

PSALM 138:2

In preparing this book, I researched what past writers have
said about the faithfulness of God. Our greatest theologi-
ans and preachers have pondered this subject for centuries. In
the 1600s, for example, a Puritan named Richard Sibbes wrote a
classic sermon on God's faithfulness, which he titled "The Saint's
Hiding Place in the Evil Day."

Since it was written four hundred years ago, I've taken the
liberty of paraphrasing a portion of his message for modern
readers.

I now want to speak about the quality of God that should move us to trust in Him, namely, that He is a faithful Creator—faithful in His nature, in His Word, and in His works. Whenever you read a promise in the Bible, you can say about it: "This is a faithful saying."

Considering, therefore, that God is so faithful, let us make special use of it. Treasure up all the promises you can of the forgiveness of sins, of protection and preservation, that He will never leave us, but be our God to death—and then consider that He is faithful in performing the same. And in every promise, single out what best suits your present condition. If you are in any great distress, think upon the mighty power of God. If you are perplexed about your directions, single out the attribute of God's wisdom and ask Him to teach you the way to go. If you are wronged, fly to His justice and say, "O God, to whom vengeance belongs, hear and help Your servant." When you are disappointed in another, retire to God and to His promises, and build upon this—that God will not fail to do anything that may do you good. God's faithfulness will never disappoint you.

You will always find in God something to support your soul in the greatest extremity that can befall you. The more we discover God is faithful, the more faithful we will be in trusting Him. We should make it a continual act, every day of our lives, to commit all we have to the Lord's disposal, and to see how He discharges that trust committed to Him upon all occasions . . . , how faithful He is in delivering us in our greatest extremities and in our worst times.[1]

Sibbes's main point remains applicable today: in stormy times we hide ourselves in the faithfulness of God until the weather changes. He didn't use Psalm 138:1–2 as his primary text, but his message perfectly reflects the theme of those verses. Psalm 138 is ascribed to David, and it's a song of praise about God's faithfulness—the saint's hiding place in difficult days.

He doesn't always keep us from trouble, but He preserves us in trouble. God's presence and assistance to support His children in trouble is invincible.

RICHARD SIBBES

CHAPTER 31

NEVER IN VAIN

"Moses was faithful as a servant in all God's house," bearing witness to what would be spoken by God in the future. But Christ is faithful as the Son over God's house. And we are his house.

HEBREWS 3:5–6

Jesus is better than anything and anyone in the Old Testament. That's the message of the book of Hebrews. This anonymous book was addressed to Hebrew Christians facing an onslaught of persecution. Some were thinking of reverting back to Judaism. But consider this, said the author: Jesus is superior to the angels of the Old Testament, superior to the priests and sacrifices of the Old Testament; He is even superior to Moses.

Moses was a faithful man who uttered prophecies that were later fulfilled. But Jesus was faithful as the fulfillment of those prophecies, and He is faithful over each of us. We are His house, over which He is utterly trustworthy.

He is worthy of our trust as we work in His church. We don't always see the results of our labor, but Isaiah 55:11 says His word doesn't return empty. The Bible says, "Your labor in the Lord is not in vain" (1 Corinthians 15:58). And Galatians 6:9 says, "At the proper time we will reap a harvest if we do not give up."

On Easter Sunday, 1921, Rev. G. H. Lang preached a sermon in northern England. He received little feedback from the message and saw no results. But years later, in a single week, several people told him the message had changed their lives.[1]

Last week, I spoke at a church in California. Afterward, a security volunteer walked me to my car. "I'm glad I have a moment to speak with you," he said. "I wanted to tell you how much your book *The Strength You Need* helped me while in Iraq. I read it thoroughly, and it thoroughly blessed and strengthened me."

"Oh," I said. "What do you do in the military?"

"I'm a Navy SEAL."

I can only praise the Lord for His faithfulness. I would never have imagined that a Navy SEAL deployed overseas would read something I'd written and be blessed for his dangerous duties.

Years ago I participated in a three-day festival in my hometown, and I placed a booth on main street filled with my books. The heat was unbearable, and the crowds never showed up. I sat there three days, and I sold three books. "I'll never do that again,"

I said. Last month I was back in my hometown. When I walked into a store, a lady came up to me asking if I was Robert Morgan. "Years ago, you set up a booth on main street and I bought your little book The Red Sea Rules. That book transformed my Christian life. In the years since, my church has gone through many of your books." I was amazed. God is faithful to bless our work even when we think the results are paltry.

Now I'm wondering about the other two books I sold that week. . . .

Christ is faithful over all of God's house—the church. He will use you and bless you more than you know. He's greater than Moses. He's greater than anyone. And He has promised your work for Him is never in vain.

Count on God's faithfulness. He assures you of His own presence with you and in you by His Spirit. Receive His assurance and reckon on His fidelity.

A. T. PIERSON

CHAPTER 32

A Bird's-Eye View of Faithfulness

*He is the Maker of heaven and earth, the sea, and
everything in them—he remains faithful forever.*

PSALM 146:6

Having lived in Nashville forty years, I'm very familiar with Dr. Ming Wang, a world-class cataract and LASIK eye surgeon in our city. He has performed more than fifty-five thousand procedures and published more than a hundred papers. Among his patients are Dolly Parton, Charlie Daniels, Kenny Chesney, Naomi Judd, and Nicole Kidman.[1]

Dr. Wang grew up in China and moved to the United States in 1982. He attended Harvard and MIT, and he was an atheist. But the more he studied medicine, the human brain, and the human eye, the more his faith in atheism eroded. Over time, he became a Christian.

"The more I learned about science," he wrote, "the more—not less—evidence I saw of God's creation and design. For example, as I was becoming an ophthalmologist and learning about the inner workings of the eye, the amazing and logical arrangement of the photoreceptors, ganglion cells, and neurons, I realized there was no way that an intricate structure such as the human eye could ever evolve from a random compilation of cells. The very complexity of the human eye is, in fact, the most powerful evidence for the existence of God."[2]

It isn't just the human eye that displays the intricacies of a mind of infinite genius. The other day I watched a hummingbird drink hovering around my Lantana bush. Its little wings were beating about one hundred flutters a second, and its tiny heart was beating twelve hundred times a minute. Hummingbirds can fly thirty miles an hour and visit three thousand flowers in a single day.[3] A hummingbird is better engineered than the Air Force's most advanced helicopter.

The writer of Psalm 146 exclaimed, "Praise the LORD. Praise the LORD, my soul. I will praise the LORD all my life. . . . He is the Maker of heaven and earth, the sea, and everything in them—he remains faithful forever" (vv. 1–2, 6).

His forever faithfulness reaches the oppressed and hungry and the prisoners (v. 7). It touches the blind and those who are bowed down (v. 8). It watches over the way of the foreigner, the fatherless, and the widow (v. 9).

And it frustrates the ways of the wicked (v. 9)!

The maker of the human eye keeps His eye on you. The designer of the hummingbird's flight through the pathless air knows the way forward. And the Maker of heaven and earth remains faithful to you forever.

Just as the seasons unfold throughout the year, just as the sun rises each morning, just as the cherry tree blossoms in spring, we can trust in God's faithfulness . . . God's faithfulness in the created world around us is a constant reminder of His faithfulness toward His people.

CHRISTINA FOX, HOMESCHOOL MOTHER AND BLOGGER

CHAPTER 33

HIS FAITHFULNESS
REACHES TO THE SKIES

God sends forth his love and his faithfulness. . . .
For great is your love, reaching to the heavens;
your faithfulness reaches to the skies.

PSALM 57:3, 10

When missionary pilot Forrest Zander wrote a memoir about his experiences, he took his title from Psalm 57:10: *His Faithfulness Reaches to the Skies.* Zander had lots of opportunities to experience God's faithfulness because every flight in his small missionary plane involved rugged mountains, dense jungles, meager airstrips, emergency missions, and unstable weather.

On one occasion, Zander and his copilot were crossing the Andes Mountains in Colombia, cruising at 16,000 feet, which required their wearing oxygen masks. As he watched the fuel gauges, he was alarmed to see the needles going down much faster than he expected. There was a problem somewhere, and Zander still had the last three ranges of the Andes to cross. He needed to refuel, but where? No commercial airport was near, and alternate airstrips were rare.

Having cleared the highest mountain peaks and passed the foothills on the eastern side, Zander quickly descended to preserve fuel and looked for a place to land. Then he spotted an airstrip right at the foot of the mountain. But what about fuel? Would they have any? Circling the airstrip, he saw containers of aviation-grade fuel—guarded by a contingent of armed soldiers. This airstrip was probably used by drug runners.

Zander had no choice but to land, and he was immediately surrounded by guards with their guns. When he explained his problem, the commander offered to give him the fuel, but as he refueled, a black cloud and storm approached. The entire group—missionaries and soldiers—fled to a protected area. It was a perfect setup. As the rain pattered on the roof, Zander read to the men from his Spanish Bible, shared the gospel with them, and left the Bible for them to study.

"Then joyfully, we departed, realizing again that our times are in the Lord's hands. Sometimes delays and problems are His way of opening doors to new opportunities to love people and to serve Him."[1]

You don't have to be a pilot to realize His faithfulness reaches to the skies. You can experience it whenever there's turbulence in your life or your energy is low. Sometimes it's when we're at the lowest that His faithfulness seems the highest.

God writes with a pen that never blots, speaks with a tongue that never slips, and acts with a hand that never fails. Bless His Name!

C. H. SPURGEON

CHAPTER 34

TELLING OUR CHILDREN OF GOD'S FAITHFULNESS

Parents tell their children about your faithfulness.

ISAIAH 38:19

I have three precious adopted grandchildren, and one is also a special-needs child who was born and abandoned in the door of a sauna in Korea. His name is Jude, and he battles physical issues and intellectual disability. He's eleven, and he FaceTimed me last night excited that he had recognized a few words in the Dr. Seuss book *Hop on Pop*.

As a rule, Jude is hyperactively happy, but he hates getting up in the morning. His first words are usually, "You're so mean! You make me get up! Me no wanna go to school."

But once he's at the bus stop, he's the star of the show. The bus driver thinks he's king of the hill. He charms his teachers, cafeteria workers, and custodians, and he pretty much gets his way in everything. With his diminutive size, round eyeglasses, quizzical smile, cocked head, and shock of black hair, he keeps the world wrapped around his finger.

Jude requires a lot of attention. He has no sense of danger, so he'll walk behind horses and in front of cars or jump off cliffs. Once in California, my daughter heard a splash, turned around, and saw Jude disappearing into a pool. She jumped in with all her clothes and saved him. Grace told me, "Pretty much everything about Jude is a study of God's intimate faithfulness. Between his medical issues and his disregard of danger, it takes all of us—plus the Lord—to care for him. But the Lord is doing the heavy lifting. He is so faithful to Jude and to us."

I've needed more of God's faithfulness with my children and grandchildren than in any other area, and I want them to know how faithful He is. The Bible tells us to declare His faithfulness to our children. May I make a few suggestions about that?

First, make sure you're excited about the Lord. Our Christian faith should give us enthusiasm, optimism, and the atmospheric emotions for a happy home. We have to work on that.

Second, let your children see you reading your Bible—and make sure it's an actual book, not a tablet or phone. There's nothing wrong with Scriptures on our electronic devices, of course. But your children might think you're reading an app or playing a video game. When they see you poring over God's Word, it makes an impression.

Third, share spontaneously and frequently what you're learning in the Bible. Deuteronomy 6 says to talk about it when you get up and when you go to bed, when you're at home or when you're on the road (v. 7). Don't beat them over the head with it. Share it with a sense of wonder and gratitude.

Fourth, fill your house and your children's hearts with great hymns of the faith. I like modern Christian music too, but the songs don't stay around very long. We need to build a hymnbook in the heads of our children, songs they'll keep with them all their lives. You might start with "Great Is Thy Faithfulness."

Fifth, attend a good, solid, biblical local church. I've become convinced elementary children should join their families for worship, sitting together, singing together, and listening to the Word of God.

Finally, go to bed a bit earlier every night. Fatigue is one of the greatest enemies to happy homes. God's faithfulness is the greatest ally we can have as we seek to build happy homes. So parents, tell your children about God's faithfulness, and then entrust them into His faithful care.

....

Remember: Faithfulness is an attribute of the fruit of the Spirit, empowered by God. So pray for it. Model it. Teach it. Celebrate it.

KURT BRUNER

CHAPTER 35

WHAT WENT WRONG?

I will sing of the LORD's great love forever; with my mouth I will make your faithfulness known through all generations.

PSALM 89:1

P salm 89 has three sections, and I've been fascinated with how the writer (Ethan the Ezrahite) unfolded his feelings. The first eighteen verses are enthusiastic praise and worship. Verses 19–37 recount God's promises to King David for an abiding dynasty. And verses 38–52 seem to ask a question—what went wrong?

Apparently, Ethan was watching his nation collapse from within and without.

When I was a young man, I thought everything would always turn out all right if I simply walked with the Lord, prayed, and persevered through trouble. I still believe that, but I've since added an adverb. Things will *ultimately* turn out all right. In the rough and tough of the here and now, things may *immediately* go wrong.

Maybe very wrong.

The three stages of Psalm 89 represent three conditions in our own lives. Sometimes we're in the first eighteen verses—joyful and worshipful. Sometimes we're reminding ourselves of God's promises, as Ethan did in the middle of this psalm. And then there are those times when we're reeling from pain, asking what went wrong.

But here's what we cannot miss. The word *faithful* occurs more often in this psalm than in any other chapter of the Bible.

- *With my mouth I will make your faithfulness known through all generations*—v. 1
- *You have established your faithfulness in heaven itself*—v. 2
- *The heavens praise your wonders,* Lord, *your faithfulness too*—v. 5
- *You,* Lord, *are mighty, and your faithfulness surrounds you*—v. 8
- *Love and faithfulness go before you*—v. 14
- *Once you spoke in a vision, to your faithful people*—v. 19
- *My faithful love will be with him.*—v. 24

- *I will not take my love from him, nor will I ever betray my faithfulness*—v. 33
- *. . . the faithful witness in the sky*—v. 37
- *. . . in your faithfulness you swore to David*—v. 49

Ethan couldn't have known how God's promises to David would be ultimately fulfilled through the coming of Jesus Messiah, Son of David. But he did know this: even when things are *wrong*, God's faithfulness is *long* and *strong*.

. . . .

God is faithful . . . He always performs what He promises. He always does as He says, speaks as He thinks, remembers what He says, never changes His mind, and always performs His word.

ROBERT TRAILL

CHAPTER 36

NONSTOP FAITHFULNESS

*So then, those who suffer according to God's
will should commit themselves to their faithful
Creator and continue to do good.*

1 PETER 4:19

I read about a woman who lived in a small English village and who prayed about every need. One day she sat at her table, asking God for her daily bread. A couple of neighborhood boys lurking nearby overheard her. They ran home, fetched a loaf of bread, and hurled it through the open window. It landed on the table in front of the woman like an airplane coming in for a landing.

"Oh, thank You, Lord!" she exclaimed. "That was quick!"

The boys snickered and were found out. When she confronted

them, they said, "The Lord didn't send you that bread. We threw it through your window."

"Oh, yes. The Lord sent it," she replied with a grandmother's wry smile. "He just let the devil deliver it."

The Lord Jesus is faithful to meet all our needs, and He uses all kinds of methods to achieve His ends. Sometimes He uses affliction. It's as if some problems, illnesses, and difficulties fly through the window and land in our laps. Peter told us that when suffering comes in the will of God, we should commit ourselves into the hands of our faithful Creator and keep on doing good (1 Peter 4:19).

This is the only time in Scripture God is specifically called our "faithful Creator," but, of course, that's exactly what He is. Difficult days and seasons of suffering don't annul that. Even when the devil attacks and we find ourselves facing spiritual warfare, He who created us to begin with is faithful in His protection, provision, and providential ordering of all the circumstances.

Satan has no answer to God's nonstop faithfulness.

Let me give you my simple acrostic for God's faithful care:

F: Full
A: Access
I: Into
T: The
H: Heavenly

F: Father's

U: Unlimited

L: Love

One of the verses of the hymn "Sweet Hour of Prayer" says, "*Sweet hour of prayer! Sweet hour of prayer! / Thy wings shall my petition bear / to Him whose truth and faithfulness / engage the waiting soul to bless. / And since He bids me seek His face, / believe His Word and trust His grace, / I'll cast on Him my every care, / and wait for thee, sweet hour of prayer.*"[1]

. . . .

> It never mattered what battle I went through—
> God proved Himself faithful to me.
>
> DAVID WILKERSON

CHAPTER 37

COLLECTING HYMNS

I will praise you with the harp for your faithfulness,
my God; I will sing praise to you with the lyre.

PSALM 71:22

My friend Suzie Alesias in Exton, Pennsylvania, told me that when she was growing up, she saw the movie *Fahrenheit 451*, in which all the books were burned and there were none left in society. The only way stories were communicated was by people sharing what they remembered from those books. That image haunted Suzie. At the time, she was taking piano lessons, and she would sit and play through the hymnbook, one hymn after another. She determined that if something like *Fahrenheit 451* ever happened, at least she would know the hymns and could share them if all our sacred music went away.

"I'm so glad I did that," she told me, "because now I remember the verses of so many hymns and they have stayed with me my whole life."[1]

One of the ways we praise God for His faithfulness is by our songs of praise. Along these lines, I'm on a personal crusade to save the great hymns of the faith. Yes, I like the new music and sing it a lot. Our contemporary music is a blessing to me—to us all. It's best appreciated when it doesn't shove aside the great hymns.

Here's my reasoning.

When we memorize and meditate on a great hymn, we're coming very close to memorizing and meditating on Scripture itself. The Scripture alone is God-breathed and infallible, but our greatest sacred songs should reflect Scripture like polished metal.

When I sing "Great Is Thy Faithfulness," for example, I'm reminding myself of the truths of Lamentations 3:23, which reveals that God's compassions are new every morning, for great is His faithfulness to us. I know the words to all three stanzas of the hymn "Great Is Thy Faithfulness" because I've been singing it for many years. It had a deep impact on me while in college, and I could never sing it in those days without weeping. It bothers me a bit that I seldom cry now when I sing it, but I believe its message as much as ever.

Many of our modern songs come and go before we can learn the lyrics, and without some abiding hymns we'll soon have a generation without any retained words of hymns fixed in their memories. That's frightening to think about.

I want to encourage everyone to begin collecting hymns. I actually keep a hymnbook by the Bible on my desk and resort to it daily. I encourage you to find the songs—ancient or modern—that most speak to you and track down the words. Sing the lyrics until you know them, and then save them on your phone or in your notebook. Create a lifetime collection of songs that praise God for all His attributes, including His faithfulness.

....

Come, Thou almighty King, / help us Thy
name to sing, / help us to praise.

EIGHTEENTH-CENTURY ITALIAN HYMN, AUTHOR
UNKNOWN

CHAPTER 38

THE REVIVAL PSALM

Love and faithfulness meet together; righteousness and
peace kiss each other. Faithfulness springs forth from
the earth, and righteousness looks down from heaven.

PSALM 85:10–11

I'm keenly interested in one particular aspect of the history of Christianity, and that's the periodic occurrence of revivals and spiritual awakenings. Many such moments have occurred, and we're badly in need of another today. In my book *100 Bible Verses That Made America*, I tell about the revivals that shaped the United States of America.

Revivals often occur in many places at once. The great 1857 revival in America was followed by a similar revival in Ireland in 1859. On Saturday, June 4, 1859, the *Banner of Ulster* newspaper reported about the spiritual excitement that filled Ulster, the epicenter of the Irish revival, sending great crowds onto the streets, seeking a relationship with Christ. A tangible sense of the presence of God brooded over the city like a heavy cloud.

The reporter wrote,

> Yesterday evening the excitement and anxiety to be present during the religious worship was almost indescribable. Half past seven was the hour appointed for the opening of the church, but long before that time, the entire neighborhood was so densely thronged that the streets became almost impassable. The building would not have contained one-fifth of the number who sought admittance . . . A strong body of the local police was stationed in the vicinity to prevent disorder and annoyance, but very little occurred of this sort.[1]

It's estimated that one hundred thousand people came to Christ during this time. Sinners cried out for mercy; families went for days without sleeping; businesses closed down; the streets were filled with weeping, singing, praying, and preaching; and the newspapers covered little else.

Psalm 85 provides a biblical pattern for praying for another revival. The writer first acknowledged God's forgiveness (vv. 1–3); then he prayed, "Restore us again, God. . . . Will you not revive us again, that your people may rejoice in you?" (vv. 4, 6).

In response, God sent forth His love and faithfulness, like

two old friends meeting in the streets. The blessings of God were poured out. "The LORD will indeed give what is good, and our land will yield its harvest" (v. 12).

How we need for the love and faithfulness of God to again meet together in the streets of our cities, like two friends igniting another great awakening for our land.

Learn to pray as the psalmist did: "Restore us again, God. . . . Will you not revive us again, that your people may rejoice in you?" (Psalm 85:4, 6).

....

Disconsolate souls among us have been revived and brought to rest in God, by a sweet sense given of His grace and faithfulness.

JONATHAN EDWARDS

CHAPTER 39

TEACH ME YOUR WAY

Teach me your way, LORD, that I may rely
on your faithfulness. . . . You, Lord, are a
compassionate and gracious God, slow to
anger, abounding in love and faithfulness.

PSALM 86:11, 15

My granddaughter Chloe was fretting about which college to attend. I didn't know the answer, but I knew Someone who did, Someone who has guided me many times throughout my life. Pulling Chloe aside, I gave her one of the old hymnbooks in my collection and showed her the index in the back. One category was for hymns of guidance. I've turned to these hymns many times and used them as prayers when needing direction—hymns such as "Savior, Like a Shepherd Lead Me" and "Guide Me, O Thou Great Jehovah."

One of my favorite guidance hymns is based on Psalm 86 and its plea, "Teach Me Your Way, Lord." It was published by Benjamin Ramsey in 1919. I wish I had space to give you all four stanzas, but I'm only going to quote the first and you can look up the others on your own. This is a stanza I easily memorized, and it often comes in handy when I need to seek God's will about some matter.

> Teach me Thy way, O Lord, teach me Thy way!
> Thy guiding grace afford, teach me Thy way!
> Help me to walk aright, more by faith, less by sight;
> Lead me with heavenly light, teach me Thy way!

God is faithful to guide us in all our decision as we yield them to Him. The psalmist said, "Teach me your way, Lord, that I may rely on your faithfulness" (Psalm 86:11).

Think of the implications of that. If we go down our own path, out of God's will and away from His plan, we cannot rely on His faithfulness. We have to rely on our own ingenuity, wisdom, and resources. But when we ask for His guidance, He leads us; and as we follow Him, we can rely on His faithfulness every step.

Isobel Kuhn talks about "the Christian privilege of thinking through a problem in the presence of the Lord."[1] That's profound. In my desk, I keep a small prayer journal (a 5½" × 8½" loose-leaf notebook), and when I have a decision to make, I jot it down at the top of the page. Every morning during my devotions, I'll take a moment to pray about it, think about it, and ask God for wisdom. In one case, it took about five years before I had the needed insight and inner peace for a decision, but when the time came, the Lord helped me know.

Some decisions, of course, have to be made quickly. But never so quickly that we can't pause and pray, "Teach me Your way, O Lord."

. . . .

> Until the race is run, until the journey's done, until the crown is won, teach me Thy way.
>
> BENJAMIN RAMSEY

CHAPTER 40

THE FAITHFUL WITNESS

Grace and peace to you from him who is, and who was, and who is to come, and from the seven spirits before his throne, and from Jesus Christ, who is the faithful witnesses, the firstborn from the dead, and the ruler of the kings of the earth.

REVELATION 1:4–5

The book of Revelation tells us about the "Fifty Final Events in World History," which is also the name of a video course I teach covering the twenty-two chapters of this last great book of the Bible.[1] It's so important to know this book, which brings to a close the story of Scripture. What if the Bible had only sixty-five books, ending with Jude? Jude is a small but important book dealing with the defense of the true gospel. But it doesn't bring the story of the Bible to a fitting conclusion. Only Revelation does that.

The very first verse of Revelation gives us its title and its purpose: "The revelation from Jesus Christ, which God gave him to show his servants what must soon take place" (1:1).

Certain events—the events of the end times—are going to soon take place, and Jesus wants us to know about them in advance. He wants to reveal, not conceal, the future.

Verses 4 and 5 contain a threefold blessing for us from God the Father, God the Son, and God the Holy Spirit.

God the Father is described as "him who is, and who was, and who is to come." In other words, He is eternal, beyond time, with no beginning, no ending, and no changing of His essence or nature. As He has been, He always will be.

God the Holy Spirit is described as the "seven spirits before the throne." A better rendering would be the sevenfold Spirit. The number seven indicates perfection, and in Isaiah 11:2, the Holy Spirit is described in seven ways.

God the Son—Jesus—is described as the "faithful witness, the firstborn from the dead, and the ruler of the kings of the earth." Jesus is utterly trustworthy in every word He speaks. As He tells us about the Golden Rule, the Good Shepherd, the Lord's Prayer, the Second Coming—anything and everything that He says—He is infallibly correct and unfailingly true. He is the faithful witness.

He is also the first to be resurrected and glorified for

eternity—the pattern for the coming resurrection of believers. And He has authority over all the dominions of the earth and will bring world history to a fitting conclusion. Thus, He is faithful to His Word, to our future, and to our world.

Famous humanitarian George Müller once said after a providential answer to prayer, "The Lord in His faithfulness helped us. Help was never more truly needed . . . nor did the help of the Lord ever come more manifestly from Himself . . . Praise the Lord for His goodness. Praise Him particularly that He enabled us to trust Him in this trying hour!"[2]

How often we echo those words in our own hearts!

Praise Father, Son, and Holy Ghost!

. . . .

Through grace my mind is so fully assured of the faithfulness
of the Lord, that, in the midst of the greatest need, I
am enabled in peace to go about my other work.

GEORGE MÜLLER

CHAPTER 41

THE FEATHER CURTAIN

He will cover you with his feathers, and under
his wings you will find refuge; his faithfulness
will be your shield and rampart.

PSALM 91:4

M any years ago, as I walked across campus, I bumped into a missionary legend—Arthur Matthews, the last missionary to escape from China after the Communist takeover in 1949.[1] I was too awed to do anything but shake his hand and chat a moment, but I knew his story.

He and his wife, Wilda, and their daughter, Lilah, were serving in China when the Bamboo Curtain fell across the land in 1949. The little family was placed under house arrest, and they could hear the executions taking place on the athletic field nearby. Each day was filled with fear, privations, and danger. They never knew when the authorities would come for them. Their funds were low, their fuel was barely enough to keep the baby warm, and their food was sparse. Every time Arthur was summoned to police headquarters, Wilda never knew if she would see him again.

In those days, the concept in Psalm 91:4 became a source of great comfort for them—"He will cover you with his feathers." Though they were behind the Bamboo Curtain, they reasoned, they were also beneath the Feather Curtain of God.

Isobel Kuhn, who later recorded their story, said, "The Feather Curtain of God falls silently. It is soft and comforting to the sheltered one; but intangible, mysterious, and baffling to the outsider."[2]

The Bible talks about this curtain with surprising frequency. Psalm 17:8 says, "Hide me in the shadow of your wings." Psalm 57:1 says, "I will take refuge in the shadow of your wings until the disaster has passed." And Jesus spoke of gathering His children together "as a hen gathers her chicks under her wings" (Matthew 23:37).

I don't know if you've ever seen how a hen can hide her chicks beneath her wings, but it's one of nature's great pictures. I saw one hen who appeared to be sitting silently in the henhouse, but when she was lifted up, a dozen chicks were tucked up beneath her, as warm and secure and hidden as they could be.

That's a picture of how God cares for us, keeping us safe and secure from all alarms. "He will cover you with his feathers. He will shelter you with his wings. His faithful promises are your armor and protection" (Psalm 91:4 NLT).

....

Under His wings I am safely abiding, / Though the night deepens and tempests are wild, / Still I can trust Him; I know He will keep me, / He has redeemed me and I am His child.

WILLIAM ORCUTT CUSHING

CHAPTER 42

His Fathomless Faithfulness

*It is good to praise the Lord and make music to
your name, O Most High, proclaiming your love
in the morning and your faithfulness at night.*

PSALM 92:1–2

According to the passage above, in the morning we're to remind ourselves of God's love; and as the light dims and the evening steals over us, we're to remember His faithfulness.

After the stress of the day, with its demands, appointments, dilemmas, conundrums, and complaints, take a moment to remember God's fathomless faithfulness. He missed nothing and will work all things for the good of those who know and love Him.

If you've failed today, confess your sin, for He is faithful and just to forgive your sin (1 John 1:9).

If you're worried about tomorrow, remember that the Lord your God is a faithful God, keeping His covenant of love to a thousand generations (Deuteronomy 7:9).

If someone has wronged or offended you today, leave it with your "faithful God who does no wrong, upright and just is he" (Deuteronomy 32:4).

If you're downcast or depressed, say, "Into your hands I commit my spirit; deliver me, LORD, my faithful God" (Psalm 31:5).

If you're anxious, find a biblical promise to grasp and remember this throughout the night: "The word of the LORD is right and true; he is faithful in all he does" (Psalm 33:4).

Are you ill? The Bible says, "Those who suffer according to God's will should commit themselves to their faithful Creator" (1 Peter 4:19).

If you've had a good day, count your blessings and remember how God's faithfulness reaches to the skies (Psalm 36:5).

If you feel lonely, give someone a call, text, or note with an encouraging word to him or her about God's faithfulness, like the psalmist who said, "I speak of your faithfulness and your saving help. I do not conceal your love and your faithfulness" (Psalm 40:10).

If you need wisdom and guidance about decisions, pray, "Send me your light and your faithful care, let them lead me" (Psalm 43:3).

If you're worried about your children or loved ones, pray, "Appoint your love and faithfulness to protect him" (Psalm 61:7).

How about ending the day with a hymn or song of praise? You can sing it, play it, or listen to it. The Bible says, "I will praise you with the harp for your faithfulness, my God" (Psalm 71:22).

And do you need a benediction for ending the day? Here's one: "May God himself, the God of peace, sanctify you through and through. May your whole spirit, soul and body be kept blameless at the coming of our Lord Jesus Christ. The one who calls you is faithful, and he will do it" (1 Thessalonians 5:23–24).

Rest well; then awaken in the morning and sing of His love!

. . . .

Every morning tell him, "Thank you for your kindness,"
and every evening rejoice in all his faithfulness.

PSALM 92:2 TLB

CHAPTER 43

THE FAITHFUL JUDGE

Let all creation rejoice before the LORD, for he comes,
he comes to judge the earth. He will judge the world
in righteousness and the peoples in his faithfulness.

PSALM 96:13

W hen we speak of God's attributes, we're referring to facts about Him—the traits that characterize His divine personality. God is holy, loving, just, eternal, all-knowing, faithful, and almighty. The number of His attributes may be infinite, and each of these attributes is unending. In ways we can't fully understand, each attribute of God qualifies all the others. For example, because God is holy, His justice is holy; His faithfulness is holy; His love is holy. Because He is eternal, His power is eternal and His faithfulness is unending.

In His essential nature with all His galaxies of qualities,

God is without beginning or ending, and He fills all dimensions known and unknown. His holiness, justice, and righteousness pervade all reality and cannot be denied, avoided, or delayed.

If all this boggles your mind, remember the old saying: a God small enough to be understood isn't large enough to be worshipped. Our majestic Lord is incomprehensible, unfathomable, clothed in light, wrapped in mystery, and veiled in glory.

He is to be feared with reverent awe.

Because of this, it's unthinkable that God could see all the evil in the world—the genocide, the senseless wars, the cruelty of humanity—without responding to it. Through the power of Calvary, everything will one day be leveled, balanced, avenged, and righted. That should make us rejoice!

"God is not dead, nor does He sleep / The wrong shall fail, the right prevail."[1]

A seventeenth-century Lutheran pastor, Johann Heermann, who sought to minister during the chaos of the Thirty Years' War, wrote a prayer that perfectly reflects the sentiments of my heart today. In German, the first line is *O Gott, du frommer Gott*. Translated into English, the opening stanza says,

> O God, Thou faithful God,
> Thou fountain every flowing,
> Without whom nothing is,
> All perfect gifts bestowing,

Grant me a healthy frame,
And give me, Lord, within,
A conscience free from blame,
A soul unhurt by sin.[2]

One day Jesus will judge the world in faithfulness. He will be faithful to His holiness, and He will deal with the source of evil and the suffering it has caused the world. He is also faithful to His love for us. Let's ask Him for a healthy frame, a cleansed conscience, and a soul that will never be at home with sin.

....

When you see a specific need in your life for faithfulness, make that a matter of prayer for the aid of the Holy Spirit and the object of concrete actions on your part. Remember that your working and His working are coextensive. You cannot become a faithful person merely by trying. There's a divine dimension. But it's also true that you won't become a faithful person without trying.

JERRY BRIDGES

CHAPTER 44

The Bruised and the Depleted

A bruised reed he will not break, and a smoldering wick he will not snuff out. In faithfulness he will bring forth justice.

ISAIAH 42:3

When we built our home in 1990, our daughters stuck whirlybird-like maple seeds in pots and later planted the seedlings in the lawn. Now the trees are taller than the house and send out their own fleets of "whirlybirds" every spring. I spend hours pulling up sprouting maples. One of them escaped my notice a year or two ago, and he grew as tall and straight as a teenager. A month ago, my friend Ben Almassi and I replanted him in the field behind our house.

"God make you thrive, little fellow," said Ben.

The next day I went down to check on the little fellow and was horrified to see every leaf gone—all stripped away. It was the little fawn that had been hanging around. He had eaten every leaf and enjoyed some of the bark. There was nothing left but a naked rod sticking out of the ground. I considered the maple a lost cause, but I put a tomato cage around him and waited.

Within days he produced a big new set of green leaves. Ben's blessing worked.

My little maple was, as the prophet Isaiah would put it (42:3), "a bruised reed"—a plant that had been damaged.

To Isaiah, a damaged plant was symbolic of people who have been bruised in life. They are "bruised reeds" because they have been wounded. They are "smoldering wicks" because they are depleted. They're almost out of fuel, running low on energy, hope, and resiliency.

I said earlier that the book of Isaiah is full of prophetic information about Christ. In this chapter—Isaiah 42—we have an incredible prediction about the tender care Jesus offers to bruised and depleted people. Here's the way the passage reads in the Living Bible, as God the Father describes His Son to us in advance:

See my servant, whom I uphold; my Chosen One in whom I delight. I have put my Spirit upon him; he will reveal justice to the nations of the world. He will be gentle—he will not shout nor quarrel in the streets. He will not break the bruised reed, nor quench the dimly burning flame. He will encourage the fainthearted, those tempted to despair. He will see full justice given to all who have been wronged. He won't be satisfied until truth and righteousness prevail throughout the earth, nor until even distant lands beyond the seas have put their trust in him. (Isaiah 42:1–4 TLB)

Have you been bruised? Are you depleted? Fainthearted? Tempted to despair? Turn your eyes to Jesus. He will faithfully tend to you. He knows how to help those needing His gentle touch.

But blessed is the one who trusts in the Lord, whose confidence is in him. They will be like a tree planted by the water that sends out its roots by the stream. It does not fear when heat comes; its leaves are always green.

JEREMIAH 17:7–8

CHAPTER 45

He Is Faithful to Forgive

If we confess our sins, he is faithful and just and will forgive us our sins and purify us from all unrighteousness.

1 JOHN 1:9

Sharon Newmann, a Canadian grandmother, wrote a little book about her life, including her testimony and her poems. She came to know Jesus as her Savior at age twelve while battling kidney disease. Two days later, while lying on her stomach in the hospital bed, she asked God to heal her if it was His will. He did so, and she was thrilled.

But Sharon's mother wasn't so thrilled. She gave Sharon the impression that she didn't love her or want her, and she was verbally abusive, turning others against her. This rejection lasted for years, leading to prolonged days of hopelessness and nights of sleeplessness. Sharon spent decades battling depression.

Eventually she was drawn into a relationship with a troubled man. "I had the mistaken belief that I could help him escape from taking drugs. I thought if I could witness to him, he would change. Well, rather than him changing, I changed and fell hook, line, and sinker into this relationship."

Sharon finally broke free from the relationship, but not from the resulting guilt. "I couldn't forgive myself, and even though I prayed to God to forgive me I just couldn't feel forgiven. Night after night, I would pray the same prayer for forgiveness."

Eventually Sharon married a wonderful man and had two children. But she still battled self-condemnation. One day she enrolled in a Bible study course. "The lesson on forgiveness was invaluable," Sharon wrote. "It explained to me that even while we are Christians, we cannot live a perfect life and we still are tempted to sin. At salvation, God forgives us for sins past, present, and future. He knows we are prone to sin because we can't be perfect in this life. When we as believers sin, we don't lose our salvation, but we lose fellowship with God until we confess our sins and get right with Him again."

The verse that started Sharon on her way out of depression was 1 John 1:9, which says, "If we [freely] admit that we have sinned and confess our sins, He is faithful and just [true to His own nature and promises], and will forgive our sins and cleanse us continually from all unrighteousness" (AMP).

After Sharon realized the totality of God's forgiveness, she learned to forgive herself and to forgive others. By God's grace, she eventually even found peace with her now-aged mother.[1]

Don't yield to the stabs of self-condemnation or the harping catcalls of self-reproach. Accept your faithful Savior's full forgiveness, and use it as a foundation for rebuilding your joy and your relationships.

....

Those who, conscious of their sins, confess them, have in Christ a Savior from whom forgiveness and cleansing from every sinful act may be freely received—not because He is indulgent and easygoing, but because He is faithful and righteous. His is faithful in that His promise is sure: those who put their trust in Him will not be let down; those who come to Him will not be cast out.

F. F. BRUCE

CHAPTER 46

IN HIS HANDS

Into your hands I commit my spirit;
deliver me, LORD, my faithful God.

PSALM 31:5

P erhaps the boy Jesus memorized Psalm 31 as a youngster. Hebrew children learned many of the psalms by heart. This one was composed by King David, and Jesus would have internalized many ideas here. It begins, "In you, LORD, I have taken refuge" (v. 1). David went on to describe the groups of people causing him trouble. Some were setting traps for him (v. 4). Some were turning from his God to worship idols (v. 6). His neighbors held him in contempt (v. 11), and some were even plotting to assassinate him (v. 13).

But throughout this psalm are powerful expressions of faith. One of them is very meaningful to me: "My times are in your hands" (v. 15). One day last year, when I went to awaken my wife, Katrina, who was battling multiple sclerosis and infections, she seemed unable to speak and looked at me without comprehending what was happening. I rushed her to Vanderbilt Medical Center, and the doctor told me she appeared to be losing her fight for life. Our three daughters raced to the emergency room, but Katrina was unconscious and fading. I said to the doctor, "Do you mind if we pray?"

He said, "No, and do you mind if I lead you?" He then prayed an earnest prayer for strength and mercy, and he offered it in Jesus' name. I resumed my place at Katrina's side, peering into her peaceful face. Suddenly she opened her eyes, saw me, and smiled. "Well, look who's back!" I shouted as the girls rushed around her. Later that day, I told my family, "Our times are in His hands."

I was able to bring Katrina home, and as we came into the house, she said, "Our times are in His hands." We had a never-to-be-forgotten month of family love before the Lord gently took Katrina home.

Verse 15 is my verse in this psalm.

But verse 5 was our Lord's special verse, the one that came to His mind as He died on the cross. In harrowing agony, He recalled Psalm 31:5: "Into your hands I commit my spirit; deliver me, Lord, my faithful God."

The Bible says, "Jesus called out with a loud voice, 'Father, into your hands I commit my spirit.' When he had said this, he breathed his last" (Luke 23:46).

And His faithful God did deliver Him.

At some point, barring our Lord's return, we'll all come to the point of death. But our times are in His hands, and into those hands we can commit our spirits—and everything else of concern to us.

··

Since we know our faithful Father will abide with us till
our journey on earth is over, we can actually be thankful
for the lengthening shadows and the setting sun.

DR. VERNON GROUNDS

CHAPTER 47

MULTIPLIED PROBLEMS

The works of his hands are faithful and
just; all his precepts are trustworthy.

PSALM 111:7

I n his book *His Faithfulness Reaches to the Skies*, missionary
pilot Forrest Zander described the year his family returned
to the United States for furlough. He wanted to pursue additional
studies before returning to South America, and he was concerned
about returning to Colombia. He could well be targeted for kid-
napping during that violent period.

Meanwhile, in the States, his dad suffered a massive stroke
that required nursing home care. Zander's wife, Margaret, fell
and broke her ankle. Their son, Alby, injured his knee playing
high school football and required surgery. Their daughter called

from the University of Illinois with news that her financial aid was being canceled for the semester.

As Zander's father recovered from his stroke, he developed heart problems. At the same time his mother had a car accident and suffered a heart attack.

"I was busy directing Wycliffe's regional office in West Chicago," he said. "I was training a new assistant, and things were going slow. On top of all this, we were very low on financial support. Wycliffe encouraged me to get out every weekend to speak in churches with the hope of raising our level of support. I was speaking every Sunday and sometimes on Wednesday nights."

Doesn't it seem to you that problems and pressures come in multiplied units? Think of a game of dodgeball with thousands of flying balls coming from all directions. You can avoid some, but you can't dodge them all, and when several strike at once, it's painful.

That's when we need Psalm 111—it is all praise, all the time. It begins, "Praise the LORD. I will extol the LORD with all my heart" (v. 1). The writer went on to remind us of God's glorious and majestic deeds. "He has shown his people the power of his works" (v. 6). His work in our lives is "established for ever and ever, enacted in faithfulness and uprightness" (v. 8).

And that's the way Zander coped with his difficult year.

"If these things could be measured on a scale, the amount

of stress at that time was close to the point where I felt like I was about to have a nervous breakdown. But I turned to the Psalms, just as I had done [during a rough patch] in Colombia. I chose to cast my cares, one by one, on the Lord. And God was faithful to bring peace and encouragement."[1]

Amid multiplied problems, there is multiplied grace and amplified faithfulness.

....

> He giveth more grace when the burdens grow greater,
> He sendeth more strength when the labors increase;
> To added afflictions He addeth His mercy,
> To multiplied trials, His multiplied peace.
>
> ANNIE JOHNSON FLINT

CHAPTER 48

God's Faithfulness to Forgive

"Return, faithless Israel," declares the LORD, "I will frown
on you no longer, for I am faithful," declares the LORD.

JEREMIAH 3:12

When we have a faithless moment, we're prone to live in perpetual shame—unless we contemplate the faithfulness of God, who forgives us and takes away the frown.

Lisa Robertson, wife of Alan Robertson of Duck Commander fame, wrote, "I cannot overemphasize the importance of learning to forgive yourself for the things that pile guilt and condemnation on you. Whether it's an abortion, an addiction, a way in which you have hurt or damaged another person, or something else, the only way to move beyond it is to forgive yourself. Otherwise, you will stay trapped in negative feelings and you may even sabotage the blessings or successes that seem possible in your life."[1]

Of course, we have to have a basis for forgiving ourselves. There is only one that truly works. We have to nail our sins to the cross of Christ and recognize the full extent of His pardoning love.

Lisa continued, "I have spent time with many young women who have been molested, had abortions, and been through other types of trauma and shame. Lots of them tell me they simply cannot get over what happened to them. Without sounding harsh, I try to help them realize that saying they cannot move beyond it is the same as saying that Jesus did not do enough for them, that something about His death on the cross is insufficient. And that is just not true. His work on Calvary is more than adequate to heal anything we have done to ourselves or that anyone has done to us."[2]

Once, when I was beating myself up over something I had done years ago, I read what Joseph said to his brothers, who had betrayed him into slavery years before: "Don't be upset or angry with yourselves *any longer* because of what you did. You see God sent me here ahead of you to preserve life" (Genesis 45:5 VOICE).

Claim those words for yourself!

Don't be upset or angry with yourself any longer!

God isn't frowning at you. Because of Jesus Christ, His countenance is on you for good. His smile is friendly because His heart is faithful.

When we once truly grasp the acidic nature of Christ's blood to dissolve every particle of sin and shame, we'll never again look backward in horror, regret, or anguish. We'll say, "Yes, I had some bad moments, but they are covered with a heavy coat of blood, and God is slowly molding me into His new version of myself, which is a miniature version of Himself. Hallelujah!

Thy faithfulness, Lord, each moment we find,
So true to Thy Word, so loving and kind.

CHARLES WESLEY

CHAPTER 49

"Just a Sweet Little Journey"

Know therefore that the Lord your God is God;
he is the faithful God, keeping his covenant of
love to a thousand generations of those who
love him and keep his commandments.

DEUTERONOMY 7:9

My mom had several siblings, all of whom knew the Lord. Aunt Mable lived in a little frame house on Buck Mountain, North Carolina, and I have childhood memories of visiting her on molasses-making day. The mule would trudge around in circles, grinding the sugarcane, and the juice would trickle into an outdoor vat, where it boiled and cooked all day. After the molasses was transferred to jars, we kids would sop up the rest with little hand-whittled paddles.

For some reason, however, I didn't get to know Aunt Mable very well.

Then, one day in 1986, I saw her at a funeral, and we sat down to chat. Aunt Mable told me about visiting her brother, my uncle Alton, on the night before he died. As she left his bedside, he told her, "I believe the Lord is going to take me home to heaven. And don't worry. It's just a sweet little journey."

The greatest theologian couldn't have said it better. When the Lord takes us to heaven, it's just a sweet little journey. But upon arriving there, think of all the family we'll meet. Not just the family of other Christian believers, but all those in our own family trees who knew Christ.

His mercy extends a thousand generations before us and after us—until He returns. I never knew my great-grandparents, and I'm eager to hear their stories. I know we had some preachers in the family tree, and I'm eager to meet them. My ancestors—and yours—go all the way back to Adam and Eve. How amazing to think of our genealogies coming to life. We'll get to know our great-great-great-great-grandparents and learn their stories of faith.

And what of those who come after us? My wife, Katrina, lived long enough to see our granddaughter, Christiana, get married in our patio. But Katrina made a sweet little journey to heaven before baby Scarlet showed up a year later. I believe they'll be buddies in the future. Katrina loved having grandkids over for afternoon tea, and I can visualize that happening every single day at three o'clock on her patio in New Jerusalem.

I'm not being sentimental and trite. I believe heaven is just as real as earth, and more so. It's described vividly for us in Scripture, and God will be faithful to every detail. His faithfulness extends backward and forward for a thousand generations—and forever in eternity.

What comfort! What hope!

....

The storms may be swirling around me, but they are not swirling within me. I have total peace. Joy. Expectancy. Trust. I know I am in God's hands . . . So before I know the outcome of the surgery, I want to praise the Lord for His great faithfulness.

ANNE GRAHAM LOTZ, BEFORE UNDERGOING BREAST
CANCER SURGERY, SEPTEMBER 18, 2018

CHAPTER 50

He Remains Faithful

If we are faithless, he remains faithful,
for he cannot disown himself.

2 TIMOTHY 2:13

The Lord is perfect in His faithfulness, but we aren't. How wonderful to know He remains faithful in all circumstances. His faithfulness isn't affected by our fickleness.

The apostle Paul wrote about this during his final imprisonment just before he was beheaded. His last known letter was sent to his son in the faith, Timothy, encouraging him to maintain his resolve to serve Christ. Right in the middle of the second chapter, Paul recorded one of his poems or hymns, which he called a "trustworthy statement."

If we died with him,
> we will also live with him;

if we endure,
> we will also reign with him.

If we disown him,
> he will also disown us;

if we are faithless,
> he remains faithful,

> for he cannot disown himself. (2 Timothy 2:11–13)

Paul's writings are dotted with poems, and I think he was a hymnist. He was providing spiritual songs for the early church, and this one was written just for Timothy. It has four thoughts.

First, we died with Christ. This is a figure of speech that recurs in Paul's letters. There's a sense in which we die to self and sin when we begin living for Christ. But if we die in Him, we will live in Him and live with Him forever.

Second, we must endure. The entire letter of 2 Timothy is Paul's shout from the rim of the grave for Timothy and for us to remain true and steady, even in the face of threats and intimidation.

Third, we must not disown Christ, as Judas Iscariot did in the Gospels.

Fourth, we're not going to be perfect until we get to heaven, but our imperfections don't mar the utter faithfulness of Jesus.

He remains faithful, for He cannot deny the promises He made or the integrity of His divine nature, which cannot sin and will not fail. This is the second time the Bible speaks of the Lord remaining faithful. The other occasion is in Psalm 146:6: "He is the Maker of heaven and earth, the sea, and everything in them—he remains faithful forever."

It's not that He *was* faithful, or that He *is* faithful. He *remains* faithful to us faltering followers, both now and forever.

If my Lord were not kind to me tonight when I go to Him with my burden, I should think that I had knocked at the wrong door, because the Lord has been so good and so faithful to me up to now that it would take my breath away if I found Him changed.

C. H. SPURGEON

CHAPTER 51

Storm Clouds

I saw heaven standing open and there before me was a
white horse, whose rider is called Faithful and True.

REVELATION 19:11

As I was about to start writing this sentence, I stepped onto
the porch to watch the remnants of a hurricane approach.
It had made its way from the Gulf of Mexico, through Louisiana,
past Arkansas, and into Tennessee. Thick ashen billows heaved
through the sky at the speed of slow-moving freight cars, and the
cloud cover was low. The wind tore at the trees, and I scanned
the horizon for a tornado. The nearby sirens didn't sound, but
sheets of rain drove me inside. It felt ominous. The leaden clouds
presaged rain, the lightning brought the thunder, and the storm
will eventually give way to . . .

Oops. The tornado sirens just went off . . .

I'm back now. Though I was talking about the weather, I could have been describing the times we're in. As we look at our fractured planet, with its wars and conflicts, its dangers and rising threats, we see storm clouds billowing toward us. Sirens are sounding, and I'm convinced we're on the verge of unfolding prophetic events.

Hallelujah, we know how it will end!

Revelation 19 is the Hallelujah chapter of the Bible, as the angels of heaven sound forth with one "Hallelujah" after another. They are heralding the return of Christ to earth. Verses 5–7 say,

> Then a voice came from the throne, saying: "Praise our God, all you his servants, you who fear him, both great and small!" Then I heard what sounded like a great multitude, like the roar of rushing waters and like loud peals of thunder, shouting: "Hallelujah! For our Lord God Almighty reigns. Let us rejoice and be glad and give him glory!"

Beginning in verse 11, we have an image of the return of Christ to earth like a rider on a white horse, galloping through the sky. His eyes will blaze fire, and many crowns will sit on His brow. The name of the rider is "Faithful and True."

One day Jesus Christ is going to faithfully and truly fulfill all the promises of His return.

Jesus said, "For as lightning that comes from the east is

visible even in the west, so will be the coming of the Son of Man" (Matthew 24:27).

He will be faithful and true to that promise.

Jesus said, "I will come back and take you to be with me" (John 14:3).

He'll be faithful and true to that promise.

Jesus said, "At that time people will see the Son of Man coming in clouds with great power and glory" (Mark 13:26).

He will be faithful and true to that promise.

Jesus said, "For the Son of Man is going to come in his Father's glory with his angels" (Matthew 16:27).

He'll be true and faithful to that promise.

Jesus said, "I am the resurrection and the life. The one who believes in me will live, even though they die" (John 11:25).

He will be true and faithful to that promise. The One who is coming again is faithful and true. That is His name, and that is His nature. We should think about His return more often than we do and anticipate it more than we are.

What if it were today?

. . . .

Everything we do should be done to God's glory so that we
will be prepared at any moment for Christ's return.

CHARLES COLSON

CHAPTER 52

I'VE MADE A DATE

These words are faithful and true.

REVELATION 22:6 NKJV

The last two chapters of the Bible were written very purposefully to give us a literal description of heaven. When I say literal, that's what I mean. Because Jesus rose literally and bodily from the dead and ascended to heaven—and because our resurrection bodies will be like His—I truly believe the gates, walls, streets, and features of the heavenly city are as concrete as any city in the universe. Well, gold—not concrete. But you know what I mean.

At a high elevation in the middle of the city is the throne of almighty God, and a river gushes from beneath the throne—the Crystal River. It flows along the great golden boulevard of the city, and a vast park extends on all directions. The actual words in Revelation 22 are,

> Then the angel showed me the river of the water of life, as clear as crystal, flowing from the throne of God and of the Lamb down the middle of the great street of the city. On each side of the river stood the tree of life, bearing twelve crops of fruit, yielding its fruit every month. . . . The throne of God and of the Lamb will be in the city, and his servants will serve him. (vv. 1–3)

Let me end this book on a personal note about my lovely wife. When Katrina was taking the "sweet little journey" ahead of me into that celestial city last November (see devotion 49), I leaned over and kissed her and whispered in her ear: "Go on to sleep, honey, and in the morning we'll take a stroll alongside the Crystal River."

I was choking back tears, but the image in my mind was as clear as day. I was making a date with her—and one day I'm going to keep it. I have no doubt about that, because verse 6 tells us the biblical description of New Jerusalem, the heavenly city, is faithful and true. Like anyone else, I have moments of grief, and I miss Katrina very much. This is the first book I've written without her. With previous books, she always read and reviewed every page, often making suggestions.

I'm sorry she's not here now. But what fun we'll have on that day when I see her again!

I want to invite you to join us there. Jesus Christ is our passport to eternity, and He alone can forgive your sins, restore your relationship to God, and give you the assurance of eternal life. He will give you strength and mercy for each day—and for *that* day.

I urge you to trust Him completely, because He is worthy of all your trust. He is trustworthy and true. Great is His faithfulness.

....

When our hearts fainted and all around us seemed to give way, then we would stay ourselves on His Word. His precious word of promise, that He would never leave us, that He would uphold and strengthen us, and that as our day, so shall our strength be. We leaned on His faithfulness. Leaning on the arm of a faithful God, we found support and were enabled to press on our way.

JAMES SMITH

Notes

CHAPTER 1: HIS FAITHFUL PROMISES

1. Rev. Joseph G. Rainsford, *The Faithfulness of God* (London: S. W. Partridge, 1882), 85.
2. Rainsford, 86.
3. Rainsford, 89–90 (paraphrased).
4. Rainsford, 30–31.

CHAPTER 2: THE DIVINE FACTS

1. Thomas Chisholm, "Great Is Thy Faithfulness," published in 1921. Copyright renewed in 1951 by Hope Publishing, Carol Stream, IL.

CHAPTER 3: HIS FAITHFUL GUIDANCE

1. Jeannie Law, "Once Struggling Actress, Filmmaker Madeline Carrol, Says God Is Faithful," *Christian Post,* February 8, 2020, https://www.christianpost.com/news/once-struggling-actress-filmmaker-madeline-carroll-says-god-is-faithful.html.

CHAPTER 5: "THIS IS A MIRACLE"

1. Leonard W. Dewitt, *Jehovah-Jireh Is His Name* (Elkhart, IN: Bethel, 1990), 14–15.

CHAPTER 9: OUT ON A LEDGE

1. Riley Zayas, "Drury University Baseball Star Clay Engel Lives for God After Miracle in Estes Park," *Sports Spectrum*, August 4, 2020, https://sportsspectrum.com/sport/baseball/2020/08/04/drury-star-clay-engel-lives-for-god-after-miracle/.

CHAPTER 10: LIVE IN RELIANCE ON HIS FAITHFULNESS

1. Leah MarieAnn Klett, "Christian 'Biggest Loser' Winner on Finding Worth Beyond the Scale," *Christian Post*, February 23, 2020, https://www.christianpost.com/news/christian-biggest-loser-winner-on-finding-worth-beyond-the-scale-purpose-in-motherhood.html.

CHAPTER 11: GOD'S INK

1. Tuan is not his real name, which I've concealed for his safety.
2. I previously told this story of Tuan in *Mature Living*, December 2020.

CHAPTER 12: "STRANGE!"

1. Dr. V. Raymond Edman, *Out of My Life* (Grand Rapids: Zondervan, 1961), 119–21.

CHAPTER 14: ENOUGH

1. Helen Roseveare, *Enough* (Ross-shire, UK: Christian Focus, 2011), 10, italics hers.

CHAPTER 17: THE DIGNITY OF HUMILITY

1. Pat Williams, *Humility* (Uhrichsville, OH: Shiloh Run Press, 2016), 13.

CHAPTER 18: THE SHORTEST CHAPTER IN THE BIBLE

1. Julie Lake, "Felt Board Faith," *Julie H. Lake* blog, June 20, 2020, http://juliehlake.com/felt-board-faith/.

CHAPTER 20: "IN ALL HE DOES"

1. Jessie Clarks, "TCB Exclusive: Jordan St. Cyr Talks Rediscovering Christ During Difficult Trials" TheChristianBeat. org, July 13, 2020, https://www.thechristianbeat.org/index.php/interviews/8001-tcb-exclusive-jordan-st-cyr-talks-rediscovering-christ-during-difficult-trials.

CHAPTER 21: CHRIST'S FAITHFULNESS IN LITTLE THINGS

1. Sinclair B. Ferguson, "The Faithfulness of Christ in Little Things," *Tabletalk* magazine, July 2019, https://tabletalkmagazine.com/article/2019/07/the-faithfulness-of-christ-in-the-little-things/. I'm indebted to Sinclair B. Ferguson for his insights.

CHAPTER 22: HE MAKES NO MISTAKES

1. A. M. Overton, "He Maketh No Mistake," stanzas 1, 2, and 5, from a book in my library, titled *The Chimes of Dawn,* by A. M. Overton (publisher and publication date unknown). See Rob Overton, "He Maketh No Mistake," *ChurchLead*, January 27, 2011, https://www.churchlead.com/mind_wanderings/view/1630/he_maketh_no_mistake.

CHAPTER 25: "ONE FOUND ONESELF STEADIED"

1. Marie Monsen, *A Present Help* (Shoals, IN: Kingsley, 2011), 59–60.

CHAPTER 27: SHELTERED BY GOD'S PROMISES

1. Sheila Walsh, *The Shelter of God's Promises* (Nashville: Thomas Nelson, 2011), 2.
2. Walsh, 8.
3. Walsh, 10–11, emphasis in original.

CHAPTER 29: THE BOOK IN THE GRASS

1. A. W. Tozer, *Jesus, Our Man in Glory* (Chicago: Moody, 1987), 53–55.

CHAPTER 30: THE SAINT'S HIDING PLACE

1. Adapted from Richard Sibbes's sermon "The Saint's Hiding Place in the Evil Day," in *The Complete Works of Richard Sibbes, D.D.: Memoir of Richard Sibbes* (London: J. Nichol, 1862), 411–20.

CHAPTER 31: NEVER IN VAIN

1. G. H. Lang, *An Ordered Life* (Shoals, IN: Kingsley Press, 1988), 84.

CHAPTER 32: A BIRD'S-EYE VIEW OF FAITHFULNESS

1. "Meet Dr. Ming Wang, MD, PhD," website of Dr. Ming Wang, accessed September 29, 2020, https://drmingwang.com/about/meet-dr-ming-wang.html.
2. Quoted by Richard E. Simmons III in *Reflections on the Existence of God* (Birmingham: Union Hill, 2019), 202.
3. Melissa Mayntz, "25 Fun Facts About Hummingbirds," The Spruce, updated September 17, 2020, https://www.thespruce.com/fun-facts-about-hummingbirds-387106.

CHAPTER 33: HIS FAITHFULNESS REACHES TO THE SKIES

1. Forrest Zander, *His Faithfulness Reaches to the Skies* (Forrest Zander, 2015), 120–22.

CHAPTER 36: NONSTOP FAITHFULNESS

1. William Walford, "Sweet Hour of Prayer" (1845), verse 3.

CHAPTER 37: COLLECTING HYMNS

1. Based on a personal conversation and used with permission.

CHAPTER 38: THE REVIVAL PSALM

1. Samuel Adams, ed., *Through Editors' Eyes: The 1859 Revival in Ireland* (Dromara, UK: Revival Publishing, 2009), 27.

CHAPTER 39: TEACH ME YOUR WAY

1. Isobel Kuhn, *Green Leaf in Drought-Time* (Singapore: OMF Books, 1997), 22.

CHAPTER 40: THE FAITHFUL WITNESS

1. For more information, see the Video Courses page on the Robert J. Morgan website, at https://www.robertjmorgan.com/studies/.
2. George Müller, *A Narrative of Some of the Lord's Dealings with George Muller* (London: J. Nisbet, 1855), 440–41.

CHAPTER 41: THE FEATHER CURTAIN

1. Specifically, the last China Inland Mission missionary.
2. Kuhn, *Green Leaf in Drought Time*, 61.

CHAPTER 43: THE FAITHFUL JUDGE

1. Henry Wadsworth Longfellow, "I Heard the Bells on Christmas Day" (1863), verse 3.

2. Johann Heermann, "O God, Thou Faithful God" (1630), translated into English by Catherine Winkworth in 1858.

CHAPTER 45: HE IS FAITHFUL TO FORGIVE

1. Sharon Newmann, *My Story Through Poetry: From Despair to Triumph!* (self-pub., 2012), locs. 105–386, Kindle.

CHAPTER 47: MULTIPLIED PROBLEMS

1. Forrest Zander, *His Faithfulness Reaches to the Skies* (Forrest Zander, 2015), 192.

CHAPTER 48: GOD'S FAITHFULNESS TO FORGIVE

1. Al and Lisa Robertson, *A New Season: A Robertson Family Love Story of Brokenness and Redemption* (New York: Howard Books, 2015), 92.

2. Robertson, 92.

ABOUT THE AUTHOR

R obert J. Morgan is a writer and speaker who serves as the teaching pastor at the Donelson Fellowship in Nashville. He is the author of *The Red Sea Rules, The Strength You Need, Reclaiming the Lost Art of Biblical Meditation, Then Sings My Soul,* and many other titles, with more than 4.5 million copies in circulation. He is available to speak at conferences and conventions. Contact him at www.robertjmorgan.com.